THE P(

WILD ⌐LⵁWERS
OF THE BRITISH ISLES AND
NORTHERN EUROPE

THE POCKET GUIDE TO
WILD FLOWERS
OF THE BRITISH ISLES AND
NORTHERN EUROPE

PAMELA FOREY

DRAGON'S
WORLD

Dragon's World Ltd
Limpsfield
Surrey RH8 0DY
Great Britain

First published by Dragon's World 1992

© Dragon's World 1992
© Text Pamela Forey 1992
© Illustrations Norman Barber, Angela Beard, Richard Bell, Alma
Hathway, Roger Kent, David More, Susanna Stuart-Smith and David
Thelwell, all of Bernard Thornton Artists, London

Editors: Trish Burgess, Diana Steedman
Editorial Director: Pippa Rubinstein
Designer: Ann Doolan
Series Designer: Dave Allen

A catalogue record for this book is available from the British Library

ISBN 1 85028 083 5

Typeset by Action Typesetting Ltd, Gloucester

Printed in Singapore

CONTENTS

Introduction

A world without plants would be a world without life, for it is plants that trap the sun's energy and make it available to animals. There are about 15,000 flowering plants in Britain and Europe, about 2500 of them widespread. They grow on hills and mountains, heaths and downs, in woods and meadows, ponds and rivers, in marshes and on coastal beaches. These are natural habitats in the main, but plants also grow in cities and waste places, on roadsides and railway embankments. They come in many different shapes, their forms linked to the places in which they live; oaks and other trees grow in the lowlands and valleys, leafy, spring-flowering plants carpet the woodland floors, heathers grow in the acid soils of moors and heaths, low-growing, calcium-loving plants form cushions on chalk downs and in the mountains, salt-resistant, water-storing plants survive the rugged life on the coasts, filmy water plants grow in ponds and streams, tough, opportunist colonists grow in wasteland.

Plants adapt to these habitats from one main form. They have roots which enable them to absorb water from the soil and which anchor them in the ground. The stem forms the body of the plant, linking roots and leaves and carrying water and nutrients to all parts. The leaves trap the sunlight in the process of photosynthesis and provide the plants with energy and food to grow. Flowering plants bear flowers, which produce the female ovules and the male pollen. Pollination results in the formation of seeds, which develop within the fruits and are then dispersed, spreading the plants to new areas of suitable habitat.

Each species tends to be adapted to, and is often confined to, a particular kind of habitat, growing in that habitat and nowhere else. It is easy to see that water plants cannot survive on land, but the land also imposes distinctions, although in a more subtle form. Often many of the plants found in a particular habitat develop similar adaptations, a response to the environment in which they grow.

Desert plants may have deep and spreading roots to tap water sources deep in the ground, stems which store water, and spines or hairs and small, thick leaves to reduce water loss. Coastal plants must withstand drying winds and must be able to grow in salt-laden soil; water is difficult to extract from such soil and coastal plants, like desert plants, frequently face water shortages; often they too have succulent stems and thick leaves. Many alpine plants hug the ground to withstand the drying winds of summer and to gain protection from snow cover in winter.

Plants which grow in meadows or woods do not need such extreme adaptations to survive in their much less harsh environments. However, these plants too have adapted. Many plants of deciduous woods have their main growing and flowering season in the spring before the light is dimmed in the heavy shade of summer; many of them die down in midsummer, surviving until the following spring by thick underground roots or bulbs which store food.

The flowering plants have not arrived at this diversity overnight. Their history goes back more than 110 million years, to a time when they began to replace Gymnosperms as dominant plants on Earth. Since then they have evolved into many different families. Some families have been highly successful, with thousands of species in many different parts of the world and in many different habitats, others have remained small and confined to specific areas.

Present-day families share features that reflect their evolutionary history. For instance, some families have a high proportion of members that are poisonous, often because they all contain similar poisonous alkaloids or other chemicals. Presumably the presence of the poisons prevented animals from eating the plants, so this became a survival characteristic — a useful feature in the competition for survival that goes on all the time among the plants and animals of our planet. Other families have a high proportion of edible members. Some families are aquatic, others form bulbs or have bristly hairs. Some families are economically important, while others are not. Some families have bright, showy flowers while others have dull ones. This often reflects a difference in pollination mechanisms, the showy flowers designed to attract insects while the dull ones rely on wind to spread their pollen.

All over the world today plants and animals are under threat as habitats are changed to suit mankind, while the needs of the native plants and animals are disregarded. Even man-made habitats like cornfields and hay meadows are now poor instead of rich in wild flowers, a result of modern farming techniques. It is becoming clear that the process of habitat destruction cannot continue indefinitely if we wish to maintain the ancient diversity of our planet on which its health seems to depend. Preservation of habitats and of species is becoming an urgent priority, one to which all who value our heritage and who would wish to preserve our future need to give their support.

Key to the Flower Families

This section will help you to identify unknown plants. The key provides a series of alternatives, the object being to lead you to one of the flower families. The number at the end of each paragaph refers you to the next paragraph you should read in your search. It is a bit like following a maze with many endings. Once you reach a family name, turn to the relevant page(s) and check there to find your plant. A floral key can look daunting, but finding a wild flower and tracking it down through a key is a very satisfying experience. Any terms which the reader might find unfamiliar are explained in the glossary at the back of the book.

1   Plants which lack chlorophyll. 2
    Green plants. 4

2   Flowers regular. **Bird's-nest fam.** p. 101, **Bindweed fam.** p. 114.
    Flowers bilaterally symmetrical. 3

3   Petals fused into a corolla-tube. **Figwort fam.** (*Lathraea*) p. 144, **Broomrape fam.** p. 144.
    Petals free. **Orchid fam.** p. 196.

4   Parasitic plants forming clumps on the branches of trees. **Mistletoe fam.** p. 14.
    Plants not as above. 5

5   Plants aquatic and free-floating. 6
    Land plants or rooted aquatic plants. 7

6   Leaves finely divided, with bladders for catching water animals. **Butterwort fam.** p. 145.

    Leaves not finely divided and lacking bladders. **Frogbit fam.** p. 181, **Duckweed fam.** p. 195.

7   Perianth of 2 whorls (sepals and petals), differing from each other in colour, shape and function. 8
    Perianth of 2 or more whorls, not markedly differing from each other, often all petal-like. 56
    Perianth of 1 whorl or perianth absent. 61

8   Petals free. 9
    Petals fused into a tube, at least at the base. 32

9   Ovary superior. 10
    Ovary inferior. 28

10   Insectivorous plants, with sticky hairs on the leaves. **Sundew fam.** p. 47.
    Plants not as above. 11

11   Flowers markedly bilaterally symmetrical. 12

Flowers more or less regular. 14

12   Fruit a pod, flowers pea-like, with a 5-lobed calyx and a corolla formed of a large standard petal at the back, 2 wing petals and 2 lower petals joined to form a keel. **Pea fam.** p. 60.
Fruit a cluster of follicles, sepals petal-like, petals forming nectaries within the sepals. **Buttercup fam.** p. 26.
Fruit a capsule or nutlet, flowers not as above. 13

13   Stamens 5, alternating with petals; sepals 3, the lowest large and spurred, lateral ones small; petals 5, upper one large, the 2 on each side joined together. **Touch-me-not fam.** p. 74.
Stamens 5, alternating with petals and the 2 lowest spurred; sepals 5 and free; petals 5, free, the lowest spurred. **Violet fam.** p. 80.
Stamens 12–25, crowded at front of flower; petals 4–7, divided, and those at back of flower larger with deeper divisions. **Mignonette fam.** p. 46.
Stamens , each one divided into 3; sepals 2, small and soon falling; petals 4, in 2 whorls, the inner ones often joined. **Fumitory fam.** p. 33.

14   Fruit of 5 sections each with a long beak and a single seed in a swelling at the base. **Geranium fam.** p. 72
Fruit not as above.   15

15   Fruit a capsule.   16
Fruit fleshy, or an achene or pod, not a capsule.   22

16   Stamens 10 or less, or 12 and twice as many as the petals.   17
Stamens numerous.   21

17   Sepals 2, free. **Purslane fam.** p. 15.
Sepals 4–5, free or united into a calyx.   18

18   Style 1. **Wintergreen fam.** p. 100.
Styles 2–5.   19

19   Stamens 5, alternating with petals, but also with 5 sterile stamens. **Flax fam.** p. 70.
Stamens 8–10, twice as many as petals.   20

20   Leaves borne in opposite pairs, simple and usually narrow. **Pink fam.** p. 20.
Leaves alternate, pinnately divided with simple leaflets jointed to stalk. **Wood Sorrel fam.** p. 70.
Leaves alternate or borne in dense rosettes, simple and often thick. **Saxifrage fam.** p. 50.

21   Sepals 2. **Purslane fam.** p. 15, **Poppy fam.** p. 34.
Sepals 3 or 5. **Rockrose fam.** p. 82.

22   Fruits single-seeded nutlets arranged in a ring cupped in the calyx. **Mallow fam.** p. 78.

Fruits a cluster (not a ring) of single-seeded achenes, or in pods, or fleshy. 23

23 Petals 3. **Crowberry fam.** p. 100, **Water-plantain fam.** p. 180.
Petals 4, 5 or more numerous. 24

24 Stipules present. **Rose fam.** p. 52.
Stipules absent. 25

25 Petals 4, in the form of a cross; fruits siliquas, with 2 valves opening from below. **Mustard fam.** p. 36.
Petals 5 or more, or if 4 then not in the form of a cross. 26

26 Evergreen woody climber; fruit a berry. **Ivy fam.** p. 87.
Herbaceous plants; fruit a cluster of follicles or achenes. 27

27 Succulent plants, with thick, fleshy, entire leaves. Stamens as many as or twice as many as petals. **Stonecrop fam.** p. 48.
Plants not succulent and leaves usually lobed or divided. Stamens numerous. **Buttercup fam.** p. 26.

28 Flowers bilaterally symmetrical. **Orchid fam.** p. 196.
Flowers more or less regular. 29

29 Flowers very small with a tiny calyx and 5 petals borne

in umbels; fruit in 2 sections joined together across the top of a central axis. **Carrot fam.** p. 88.
Flowers not in umbels, or if so, fruits not as above. 30

30 Stipules present; stamens numerous. **Rose fam.** p. 52.
Stipules absent or soon falling; stamens 10 or less. 31

31 Styles 2. **Saxifrage fam.** p. 50.
Style 1. **Dogwood fam.** p. 87, **Willowherb fam.** p. 84.

32 Ovary superior. 33
Ovary inferior. 46

33 Flowers regular. 34
Flowers bilaterally symmetrical. 41

34 Flowers tiny, green and inconspicuous, in spikes. Stamens conspicuous with long filaments and large anthers. **Plantain fam.** p. 146.
Flowers not as above. 35

35 Stamens twice as many as petals or petal-lobes. **Stonecrop fam.** p. 48, **Heath fam.** p. 98.
Stamens as many as petals or petal-lobes. 36

36 Stamens opposite petal-lobes. 37
Stamens alternating with petal-lobes. 38

37 Sepals 2, overlapping, free or united. **Purslane fam.** p. 15.

Sepals joined into tubular calyx which has 5–10 ribs, expanding and membranous at the top; styles 5. **Sea Lavender fam.** p. 106.

Sepals joined into a tubular, toothed or lobed, often leafy, not membranous calyx (usually with 5, sometimes up to 9, lobes or teeth); style 1. **Primrose fam.** p. 102.

38 Fruit 2 or 4 nutlets. **Forget-me-not fam.** p. 116.

Fruit a follicle. **Dogbane fam.** p. 106.

Fruit a capsule. 39

39 Sepals free. **Bindweed fam.** p. 114.

Sepals joined into a 5-lobed calyx. 40

40 Ovary 1-celled. **Bogbean fam.** p. 107, **Gentian fam.** p. 108.

Ovary 2-celled. **Nightshade fam.** p. 122.

Ovary 3-celled. **Phlox fam.** p. 114.

41 Flower with 4 petals, outer 2 spurred, joined at tips, inner 2 often joined; stamens 2, each one divided into 3. **Fumitory fam.** p. 33.

Flower not as above. 42

42 Flowers pea-like, with a 5-lobed calyx and a corolla formed of a large standard petal at the back, 2 wing petals and 2 lower petals joined to form a keel. Fruit a pod. **Pea fam.** p. 60.

Flowers not as above. 43

43 Flowers with 5 free sepals, 3 outer ones small, 2 large inner ones modified into coloured wings, and 3 petals joined together. **Milkwort fam.** p. 75.

Flowers not as above. 44

44 Stems square in cross-section, at least near the top; fruit of 4 nutlets. **Vervain fam.** p. 121, **Mint fam.** p. 124.

Stem round in cross-section; fruit a capsule. 45

45 Insectivorous plants with rosettes of soft, fleshy leaves; stamens 2. **Butterwort fam.** p. 145.

Plants not insectivorous; stamens 4 or 5. **Figwort fam.** p. 134.

46 Flowers more or less regular. 47

Flowers markedly bilaterally symmetrical. 54

47 Flowers in 4-sided heads, formed from 1 flower on each side and 1 on top. **Moschatel fam.** p. 151.

Flowers not as above. 48

48 Flowers in heads with involucre of bracts beneath; fruits dry, 1-seeded achenes. 49

Flowers not in heads as above, or if flowers in heads, then fruit a capsule. 50

49 Stamens 2 or 4, .ee. **Teasel fam.** p. 150.

Stamens 5, anthers united around the style. **Daisy fam.** p. 154.

50 Climbing plants with male and female flowers on separate plants. Stamens 5, with 2 pairs joined by their filaments and 1 free. **Cucumber fam.** p. 96.
　　Flowers hermaphrodite, or if flowers unisexual, then plant not climbing. 51

51 Stamens twice as many as petals or petal-lobes. **Heath fam.** p. 98.
　　Stamens as many as or fewer than petal-lobes. 52

52 Leaves alternate. **Bellflower fam.** p. 152.
　　Leaves opposite or in whorls. 53

53 Stamens 1–3, inserted at base of 5-lobed corolla. **Valerian fam.** p. 149.
　　Stamens 4, alternating with 4 petal-lobes. **Bedstraw fam.** p. 110.
　　Stamens 5, alternating with 5 petal-lobes. **Honeysuckle fam.** p. 148.

54 Sepals 3, petals 3, one of them forming a lip. **Orchid fam.** p. 196.
　　Flowers not as above. Sepals united to form a toothed calyx, or calyx forming a ridge; corolla 2-lipped, with 5 lobes. 55

55 Fruit a berry. **Honeysuckle fam.** p. 148.

Fruit a 1-seeded nut. **Valerian fam.** p. 149.

56 Perianth petal-like, of many similar whorls, petals becoming smaller towards the centre of the flower. **Water-lily fam.** p. 32.
　　Perianth petal-like, formed of 2 similar whorls not markedly different from each other. 57

57 Stamens numerous. **Buttercup fam.** p. 26.
　　Stamens 9 or less. 58

58 Ovary superior. 59
　　Ovary inferior. 60

59 Stamens 9; fruit formed of partly fused follicles. **Flowering Rush fam.** p. 180.
　　Stamens 6; fruit a berry or capsule. **Lily fam.** p. 182.

60 Stamens 1 or 2, borne with 3 stigmas on a special structure, the column; 1 petal forming a hanging lip. **Orchid fam.** p. 196.
　　Stamens 3. **Iris fam.** p. 190.
　　Stamens 6. **Daffodil fam.** p. 189.

61 Tall, marginal aquatic plants with thick, sword-shaped leaves and flowers in dense, terminal, green or brown, cylindrical spikes, males above and females below. **Bulrush fam.** p. 193.
　　Plants not as above. 62

62　Aquatic plants with strap-shaped or ribbon-like leaves; male and female flowers borne in separate, globular heads, males above and females below. **Bur-reed fam.** p. 192.

Land plants, or if aquatic plants, then flowers not as above. 63

63　Fully aquatic plants with submerged or floating stems and leaves in whorls, flower spikes emerging from the water. **Water-milfoil fam.** p. 83, **Mare's-tail fam.** p. 83.

Land plants, or marginal aquatic plants with both leaves and flowers emerging from the water. 64

64　Flowers in dense cylindrical spikes, either hermaphrodite and growing at an angle at the side of the stem, or unisexual with males at the top, females below and the spike sheathed in a spathe. **Arum fam.** p. 194.

Flowers not as above. 65

65　Flowers minute; male and female flowers separate but on same plant, and consisting of 1 stamen and 1 carpel. **Spurge fam.** p. 76.

Flowers not as above. 66

66　Climbing plants. 67
Herbaceous plants. 69

67　Flowers unisexual. **Yam fam.** p. 192.

Flowers hermaphrodite. 68

68　Flowers bilaterally symmetrical, each with a rounded, swollen base, a long tube and an expanded tip. **Birthwort fam.** p. 14.

Flowers regular. **Buttercup fam.** (*Clematis*) p. 29.

69　Leaves with distinctive sheathing stipules (ochreae) at base of leaf stalk. **Dock fam.** p. 16.

Stipules absent or not as above. 70

70　Flowers green and tiny, borne in spikes or in leaf axils, often dangling; male and female flowers often separate. 71

Flowers not green and tiny. 72

71　Stipules present. **Nettle fam.** p. 14, **Spurge fam.** (*Mercurialis*) p. 76.

Stipules absent. **Goosefoot fam.** p. 18.

72　Stamens numerous. **Buttercup fam.** p. 26.

Stamens 6, ovary superior. **Lily fam.** p. 182.

Stamens 6, ovary inferior. **Daffodil fam.** p. 189.

Nettle family

Urticaceae Herbs and shrubs with about 45 genera and 550 species, mostly from the tropics. Many have stinging hairs on stems and leaves.

Family features Flowers unisexual, tiny. Calyx has 4 or 5 lobes; petals 0; stamens opposite calyx lobes; ovary superior. Fruits are achenes or drupes. Leaves simple, opposite or alternate. Stipules usually present.

Stinging Nettle, *Urtica dioica*, grows in waste places, hedges and woods throughout the British Isles and Europe. It is a perennial plant with four-angled stems about 1–2m (3–6ft) tall and opposite, toothed leaves, all with stinging hairs. In summer clusters of tiny, greenish flowers grow in the leaf axils, males and females on separate plants. Nettle leaves are edible and rich in vitamins and minerals.

Stinging Nettle
Urtica dioica

Birthwort family

Aristolochiaceae About 7 genera and 400 species of vines and herbs, found in tropical and temperate areas.

Family features Hermaphrodite, usually bilaterally symmetrical flowers grow in the leaf axils. Calyx 3-lobed, often tubular, often coloured like a corolla; petals tiny or absent; stamens 6 or 12; ovary usually inferior with 4–6 cells. Fruits are capsules. Leaves alternate, simple, without stipules.

Birthwort, *Aristolochia clematitis*, is a foetid, perennial plant with erect stems up to 80cm (30in) tall and broad, heart-shaped leaves. The flowers are dull yellow, like curved tubes, each with a flared, brownish opening and a swollen base. Although poisonous, the plant has

Birthwort
Aristolochia clematitis

been used since ancient times to induce abortion and birth. It grows in cultivated land and hedges in many parts of Europe, but is rare in Britain.

Mistletoe family

Loranthaceae Semi-parasitic shrubs with about 30 genera and 400 species, from tropical and temperate areas.

Mistletoe, *Viscum album*, is one of three European species in this family, found throughout much of Europe, and in England and Wales in Britain. It grows on deciduous trees, often on apples, forming an evergreen clump of branched stems with leathery, opposite leaves. In spring its tiny flowers appear, males and females on separate plants. Female plants produce poisonous, white, sticky berries by winter, when they are cut for Christmas decorations.

Mistletoe
Viscum album

Purslane family

Portulacaceae About 17 genera and 200 species of herbs, mainly from North and South America.
   Family features Flowers regular, hermaphrodite. Sepals 2, free or united; petals 4–6, free or united; stamens 4–6 and opposite the petals, or many; ovary usually superior. Fruits are capsules. Leaves entire, alternate or opposite. Stipules bristly or papery.

Spring Beauty, *Montia perfoliata*, has been introduced into Europe and Great Britain to become locally abundant in cultivated and waste land. It forms small, annual clumps of fleshy, spoon-shaped leaves and its flowering stems end in bowl-like disks (formed from fused leaves), with clusters of small, pinkish flowers in their centres.

Spring Beauty
Montia perfoliata

Dock family

Polygonaceae Herbs or shrubs, with about 40 genera and 800 species, mainly found in temperate regions of the world. Several are garden plants, others are invasive weeds. A few, like Buckwheat and Rhubarb, are food plants.

Family features Flowers small and regular, often borne in conspicuous inflorescences. Perianth segments 3–6, and may look like petals or sepals; stamens 4–9; ovary superior. Fruits hard, dry achenes often enclosed in perianth segments. Leaves usually alternate and simple with distinctive sheathing stipules (or ochreae).

Water-peppers are a large group of species in the genus *Polygonum*, mainly from temperate regions of the world. **Redshank**, *P. persicaria*, grows beside ponds, in damp waste places and cultivated ground, beside tracks and on roadsides, throughout Europe and the British Isles. It is a smooth, hairless, annual plant, 25–75cm (12–30in) tall, with branched, reddish stems, swollen above each node, and small, lance-shaped leaves, each with a single black blotch. Its pink flowers grow in dense, cylindrical spikes on erect, leafless stems. Its young leaves can be eaten in salads or as a vegetable.

Knotgrass, *Polygonum aviculare*, is a ubiquitous weed found throughout much of the world. It grows in lawns, streets and waste ground, also on seashores. It is a hairless annual, often forming more or less prostrate mats, with branched stems up to 2m (6ft) long. It has small, linear or lance-shaped leaves with silvery, jagged ochreae and clusters of small, pinkish flowers in the leaf axils.

Redshank
Polygonum persicaria

Knotgrass
Polygonum aviculare

There are many **Docks** and **Sorrels**, *Rumex* species, in Europe. **Sheep Sorrel**, *R. acetosella*, grows in acid soils in grassland, heaths and cultivated land throughout the British Isles and Europe. It is a perennial, with leaves like spearheads and erect flowering stems up to 30cm (1ft) tall. Male and female flowers grow on separate plants, in whorls on the flowering stems. The fruits are small, three-sided, golden brown nutlets, conspicuous in masses. Common Sorrel, *R. acetosa*, is a larger plant, up to 90cm (3ft) tall. As in many members of the family, the perianth segments enlarge in fruit to become heart-shaped and winged, red-brown with conspicuous veins. This plant grows in grassy places on neutral soils throughout the British Isles and Europe. Its sour leaves can be used in salads or in sauces for fish.

Curled Dock, *Rumex crispus*, is one of the commonest weeds in the British Isles and Europe, found in waste and grassy places, on shingle beaches and cultivated land. Its leaves are a remedy for nettle stings and were at one time also used to dress burns. They grow up to 30cm (1ft) long and have curly edges. The flowering stems reach 1m (3ft) tall, with whorls of greenish flowers followed by three-angled, veined, green fruits. Each has three red tubercles, one larger than the others.

Broad-leaved Dock, *Rumex obtusifolius*, is another common weed of disturbed places, field edges and hedgerows throughout the British Isles and much of Europe. It is similar to Curled Dock but the edges of its broad leaves are wavy, not curly, and there is only one large red tubercle on each three-angled fruit.

Sheep Sorrel
Rumex acetosella

Curled Dock
Rumex crispus

Broad-leaved Dock
Rumex obtusifolius

Goosefoot family

Chenopodiaceae About 100 genera
and over 1400 species of herbs and
shrubs, found throughout the world.

Family features Flowers borne in
leaf axils or with bracts in spikes. They
are small or minute, often green,
hermaphrodite or male and female
separate. Sepals 3–5, fused; petals 0;
stamens as many as and opposite the
sepals; ovary usually superior. Fruits are
tiny nuts. Leaves are simple, alternate
and lack stipules.

Goosefoots, *Chenopodium* species, are
annual or perennial plants, many with
large, lobed leaves and spikes of reddish
or greenish, hermaphrodite flowers,
each spike formed from many flower
clusters. Young leaves and shoots of
Good King Henry, *C. bonus-henricus*,
are rich in minerals; shoots can be eaten
like asparagus, and leaves in salads.
This plant grows in farmyards, pastures
and on roadsides throughout most of
Europe — in England, Wales and
southern Scotland, rarely elsewhere in
Britain or in Ireland. It is an erect
perennial plant up to 60cm (2ft tall),
with broadly triangular leaves powdered
with meal on the undersides when
young. In summer small, greenish
flowers appear in leafless spikes in the
leaf axils.

Good King Henry
Chenopodium bonus-henricus

Oraches, *Atriplex* species, are often
difficult to distinguish from goosefoots
but have separate male and female
flowers. **Common Orache**, *A. patula*,
is an annual weed found in cultivated
ground and waste places throughout the
British Isles and Europe, particularly
near the sea. It has triangular or arrow-
shaped leaves often covered with white
hairs and its female flowers are enclosed

Common Orache
Atriplex patula

in two diamond-shaped bracts which persist around the fruits. Its leaves have a good flavour and are high in Vitamin C; they can be eaten as a vegetable.

Many members of this family grow on the coast. **Sea Beet** is a subspecies of the plant which has given rise to Beetroot and Spinach, *Beta vulgaris*; it is *B. vulgaris* subsp. *maritima*. It grows around the British and European coasts, on shingle beaches and the edges of salt marshes, in grassy places and on sea walls. It is usually biennial with sprawling, reddish stems and red-tinged, leathery, rhombic leaves. Its green flowers are borne in whorls of three in branched spikes and are followed by fruits within persistent brown petals.

Sea Beet
Beta vulgaris
subsp. *maritima*

Sea Purslane, *Halimione portulacoides*, forms colonies near the high tide mark, around estuaries and on the margins of channels in salt marshes on the coasts of England, eastern Ireland and Europe, north to Denmark. It is a creeping shrub, 80–90cm (2–3ft) tall, with sprawling, leafy stems, silvery in appearance from the tiny silver scales on its fleshy, elliptical leaves. In late summer it bears dense yellow flower spikes with male and female flowers separate. The fruits are enclosed in knobbly, yellow, three-lobed bracts.

Sea Purslane
Halimione portulacoides

Glasswort, *Salicornia europaea*, grows in sandy mud on salt marshes around the coasts of the British Isles and Europe. It is a succulent, rather translucent, annual plant with jointed, branched, erect stems. Its leaves are opposite, joined along their margins and form the 'segments'. Plants may be green or flushed with yellow and red. They can be eaten raw in salads or cooked in soups.

Glasswort
Salicornia europaea

Pink family

Caryophyllaceae About 70 genera with 1750 species of herbs. A family with many garden plants, including pinks and carnations. Some, like chickweeds and corncockle, are weeds.

Family features Flowers solitary or in cymes; regular, usually hermaphrodite. Sepals 4 or 5, free or united into a tube, often with papery margins; petals 4 or 5, sometimes 0; stamens up to 10, often twice as many as the petals; ovary superior. Fruits are dry capsules. Leaves entire, opposite and often connected by a transverse line; stipules frequently absent but when present are often papery.

Maiden Pink
Dianthus deltoides

Pinks and **Carnations** are members of the large genus *Dianthus*, with many species in Europe. Most are perennial plants with clumps of blue-green, linear leaves and attractive flowers. **Maiden Pink**, *D. deltoides*, has short leafy, non-flowering shoots and sprawling flowering shoots that lie on the ground, then turn upwards to grow 45cm (18in) tall with small, rose-coloured, spotted flowers terminating the stems. This plant grows on dry, grassy banks, in dry pastures, old quarries and near the sea, usually on chalk or limestone. It is decreasing in numbers, but is still found locally throughout Great Britain and in most of Europe.

Soapwort, *Saponaria officinalis*, has erect stems 30−90cm (1−3ft) tall with dark green, opposite leaves and terminal clusters of delicately scented, pink flowers. This plant grows in many grassy places and hedgerows in England and Wales, northwards to Aberdeen and into Scandinavia in Europe; it was probably introduced to many of these

Soapwort
Saponaria officinalis

areas. Its name comes from the soapy liquid which can be obtained from boiling its stems, used at one time for washing wool and woollen cloth.

Campions and **Catchflies** are members of the genera *Silene* and *Lychnis*. There are about 300 *Silene* and 15 *Lychnis* species, the majority from temperate areas of the world. **Red Campion**, *Silene dioica*, is an attractive but short-lived perennial plant with many non-flowering shoots and flowering shoots up to 90cm (3ft) tall in early summer. These bear soft, hairy, opposite leaves and rose-red flowers with cleft petals. Male and female flowers are separate. Plants grow in woods and hedgerows, also on limestone screes and coastal cliffs throughout much of Europe and the British Isles.

White Campion, *Silene alba*, is a sticky-hairy plant with pointed leaves and white flowers. It grows in hedgerows and grassy places, cultivated and waste land throughout lowland areas of the British Isles and Europe. White Campions and Red Campions hybridize freely, producing offspring with pink flowers. **Bladder Campion**, *S. vulgaris*, grows in cultivated land, waste and grassy places throughout the British Isles and Europe. Its flowers have veined, bladder-like calyces and deeply cleft white petals.

Ragged Robin, *Lychnis flos-cuculi*, has sprawling, leafy non-flowering shoots and erect flowering shoots about 75cm (30in) tall, the latter bearing 'ragged', rose-red flowers around midsummer. The petals are dissected into linear segments. This plant grows in damp meadows, marshes and wet woods and fens throughout the British Isles and Europe.

Red Campion
Silene dioica

White Campion
Silene alba

Ragged Robin
Lychnis flos-cuculi

Pink family

Like many stitchworts and chickweeds, **Greater Stitchwort**, *Stellaria holostea*, has short non-flowering shoots and taller flowering shoots, in this species reaching 60cm (2ft) tall. It flowers in early summer, bearing bright, satiny-white flowers with petals cleft for half their length. The flowering shoots are brittle and straggling, often supported by other plants in the rough, shady woods and hedgerows where this plant most often grows. It is found throughout the British Isles and much of Europe, north to southern Scandinavia, but rarely in the south.

Lesser Stitchwort, *Stellaria graminea*, grows in grassy places, hedgerows and woods throughout most of the British Isles and Europe. It is a perennial plant with numerous slender non-flowering shoots; these are brittle, sprawling and much-branched with grass-like leaves. In summer the branched flowering shoots bear numerous small white flowers with deeply cleft petals.

Common Chickweed, *Stellaria media*, is a ubiquitous weed of gardens, woods, waste and cultivated land; it is an annual plant, germinating in autumn, growing through the winter and flowering from early spring to late autumn. It forms a sprawling clump of weak, leafy stems no more than 40cm (15in) high, with many tiny white flowers in terminal, leafy cymes. Common Chickweed is often recommended for salads but has a fibrous texture and bitter taste and is better boiled briefly and eaten as a cooked vegetable. The plant can be identified by the line of hairs that runs down the stem from node to node.

Greater Stitchwort
Stellaria holostea

Lesser Stitchwort
Stellaria graminea

Common Chickweed
Stellaria media

Water Stitchwort, *Myosoton aquaticum*, grows in ditches and marshes, beside streams and ponds, in damp woods and other wet places throughout Europe, mainly in central and southern England in the British Isles. It is a perennial plant with fragile, straggling non-flowering and flowering shoots, stickily hairy towards the tops, and with pointed-ovate, often heart-shaped leaves. White flowers appear in loose clusters in late summer; their petals are twice as long as the sepals and cleft to the base.

Water
Stitchwort
Myosoton aquaticum

Mouse-ear Chickweeds, *Cerastium* species, can be distinguished from Stitchworts, *Stellaria* species, because Mouse-ear flowers have three styles whereas Stitchworts have five. Mouse-ear Chickweeds are so called because the short, downy hairs on the leaves of some of them resemble the fur on the ears of mice. Some are common weeds of short grassland, lawns and bare ground.

Common
Mouse-ear
Chickweed
Cerastium fontanum

Common Mouse-ear Chickweed, *Cerastium fontanum*, is a weed of grassy places, roadsides and wasteland, sand-dunes and cultivated ground, a perennial creeping plant rooting at the nodes. Its non-flowering shoots remain less than 15cm (6in) tall but flowering shoots turn upwards to reach 45cm (18in) in height. The stems are sticky-glandular and hairy, with opposite, grey-green, hairy leaves. The flowers grow in terminal, equally branched clusters; each has five hairy sepals, and five cleft white petals just a little longer than the sepals. **Field Mouse-ear Chickweed**, *C. arvense*, is another common weed of dry grassland, found throughout Europe and the British Isles. It has flowers with petals twice as long as the sepals.

Field Mouse-ear
Chickweed
Cerastium arvense

Pink family

Procumbent Pearlwort
Sagina procumbens

Thyme-leaved Sandwort
Arenaria serpyllifolia

Sea Sandwort
Honkenya peploides

Some members of this family are insignificant plants with small, often inconspicuous flowers. **Pearlworts**, *Sagina* species, carry this tendency to an extreme. They form mats of green stems with little, linear leaves, the whole plant no more than a few centimetres across and 10cm (4in) tall. **Procumbent Pearlwort**, *S. procumbens*, is a perennial weed that grows in damp places, often in lawns and paths, in damp arable land and beside streams throughout much of Europe and the British Isles. It has minute greenish flowers in the leaf axils, each with four sepals and often lacking petals.

Thyme-leaved Sandwort, *Arenaria serpyllifolia*, is somewhat similar to Common Chickweed. It is a sprawling annual plant, sometimes prostrate, with many stems and tiny, opposite, pointed-ovate leaves. However, it is wiry and rough to the touch, not succulent and not edible. Its white flowers have five uncleft petals. This plant is often found on bare ground, on roadsides and in waste places, in gardens and arable land, on walls, heaths and downs throughout the British Isles and Europe.

Sea Sandwort, *Honkenya peploides*, is a much larger species — a coastal plant found on beaches and sand-dunes around the coasts of the British Isles and Europe. It forms dense colonies with thick stems which run in and along the sand, helping to stabilize the shifting grains. Its stems have fleshy leaves arranged in four overlapping ranks, and it bears small whitish flowers in the leaf axils. Male and female flowers grow on separate plants, female flowers with minute petals.

Corn Spurrey, *Spergula arvensis*, is an annual weed growing in acid soils on cultivated land throughout the British Isles and Europe. It is also found on open ground in waste places and on roadsides. This plant is easy to spot, with slender green stems and fleshy, linear leaves which are opposite, but so divided that they look as if they are in whorls. It grows up to 40cm (15in) tall and in summer bears many terminal clusters of white flowers.

Corn Spurrey
Spergula arvensis

Sand Spurrey, *Spergularia rubra*, is a small, usually annual plant with much-branched, often prostrate stems and linear leaves. It bears clusters of small pink flowers at the ends of the stems, the five petals of each flower alternating with the sepals and shorter than them. Sand Spurrey grows in lime-free sandy or gravelly soils on tracks and fields throughout Europe and Great Britain, very locally in Ireland. Lesser Sea-spurrey, *S. marina*, is a small annual plant with mats of fleshy, prostrate stems only 20cm (8in) long, whorls of linear leaves and small pink flowers. It is one of several *Spergularia* species growing on the coast, this one in salt marshes; it may also be found on the sides of major roads treated with salt in winter.

Sand Spurrey
Spergularia rubra

Annual Knawel, *Scleranthus annuus*, is another small annual plant, this one with sprawling, branched stems up to 25cm (10in) tall, and a spiky appearance coming from the narrow, pointed leaves. It flowers around midsummer, with clusters of tiny, greenish, petal-less flowers hidden by bracts in the leaf axils. It grows in dry, sandy places, in waste ground and cultivated land throughout Europe and Great Britain, locally in Ireland.

Annual Knawel
Scleranthus annuus

Buttercup family

Ranunculaceae About 50 genera and 1900 species of herbs, shrubs and climbers found mostly in temperate and Arctic areas of the northern hemisphere. There are many garden plants in the family, including anemones, columbines and delphiniums. All members are poisonous to a greater or lesser degree.

Family features Flowers solitary or in terminal inflorescences; regular and hermaphrodite, often with all parts free. Sepals 5–8, often overlapping, sometimes petal-like; petals often 5 but may be absent or numerous, frequently overlapping, often with a nectary at the base; stamens numerous, sometimes petal-like; ovary superior, with 1 to many free carpels. Fruits are follicles or achenes. Leaves usually alternate or in a basal clump, often compound or divided. Stipules usually absent.

Monkshoods, *Aconitum* species, are perennial plants with clumps of large, palmately cleft leaves and flowering stems up to 1m (3ft) tall, bearing showy blue or yellow flowers in summer. Each flower has five petal-like sepals, the upper forming a helmet-shaped hood hiding two nectaries, remnants of the petals; each is followed by 2–5 pods.

Rhizomes of the **Monkshood**, *Aconitum napellus*, contain an alkaloid used in treating rheumatism, sciatica and inflammations. However, the plant is so poisonous that it can only be used under medical supervision. Its leaves are palmately lobed with linear segments and it has blue-mauve flowers. Monkshood grows in damp mountain meadows and woods across much of Europe, except the north, in south-western England and Wales in Britain.

Monkshood
Aconitum napellus

Stinking Hellebore
Helleborus foetidus

Stinking Hellebore, *Helleborus foetidus*, is one of several European hellebores. It is a foetid perennial plant with leafy stems which persist over the winter, dying back when new stems appear in late spring. The leaves are dark green and palmately lobed with narrowly lance-shaped, toothed segments. In early spring drooping, one-sided clusters of pale green, bell-shaped flowers appear above the leaves; they are followed by green pods. Plants grow wild in woods and rocky places in western and southern Europe, in southern and western England and in Wales, but have also become naturalized in other areas.

Marsh Marigold, *Caltha palustris*, is a hairless, perennial plant only 60cm (2ft) tall, forming a clump of long-stalked, dark green leaves with large, heart-shaped blades. Many bright yellow flowers grow on the branched stems in spring, each one with up to eight petals, 100 stamens and 5–12 carpels which enlarge into pods. Plants grow in marshy meadows, wet woods and fens, along the edges of streams and ditches throughout Europe and the British Isles.

Marsh Marigold
Caltha palustris

Globe Flower, *Trollius europaeus*, has bowl-shaped, golden flowers, each with about 10 petal-like sepals. Inside are the strap-shaped, nectar-producing petals, somewhat resembling the stamens. The flowers grow at the tops of stems 60cm (2ft) tall, hovering over the clump of long-stalked, palmately lobed leaves in early summer. They are followed by clusters of pods. Plants usually grow in mountain areas, in wet meadows, woods and marshes across much of Europe, in Wales, Scotland, northern England and northern Ireland.

Globe Flower
Trollius europaeus

Buttercup family

Herb Christopher
Actaea spicata

Herb Christopher, *Actaea spicata*, is a perennial, foetid plant, not unlike the Japanese Anemones grown in gardens. It has a clump of long-stalked leaves with large, serrated leaflets. In early summer the flowering stems develop, each with a terminal raceme of flowers. These have white sepals and petals which soon fall, leaving the white stamens still conspicuous. Unusually in this family, the fruits are berries, green at first ripening to glossy black. These are poisonous, like the rest of the plant.

There are about 120 species of **Anemones**, genus *Anemone*, mostly found in the northern hemisphere. They are usually small perennial plants with a clump of palmately divided leaves and flowers borne on separate stems. The flowers lack petals, although this is not immediately evident as the sepals resemble petals. The numerous carpels enlarge in fruit to form achenes.

Wood Anemone
Anemone nemorosa

Wood Anemone, *Anemone nemorosa*, is found in deciduous woods throughout Europe, Great Britain and Ireland, often forming large colonies. Its erect stems appear in spring, each with a whorl of three leaves and one white flower. Once the flowers are over the basal leaves appear, long-stalked and palmately lobed, dying by midsummer.

Hepatica
Hepatica nobilis

Hepatica, *Hepatica nobilis*, grows in mountain woods and copses across much of continental Europe but is absent from Britain. It is a low-growing, hairy perennial, only 15cm (6in) tall, with a clump of lobed, evergreen leaves and solitary, blue-violet flowers on long stalks in spring. The flowers lack petals and have 6–10 petal-like sepals.

Clematises, *Clematis* species, are unusual among members of this family in that many are climbers; they include some of the most popular garden plants. **Traveller's Joy**, *C. vitalba*, climbs with twining stems up to 30m (100ft) tall, in woodland edges, hedgerows and thickets, on calcareous soils throughout much of Europe from Holland southwards, and in England and Wales. It has compound leaves with three or five pointed-ovate, toothed leaflets and clusters of fragrant flowers in the leaf axils in summer. Each flower has four greenish-white, petal-like sepals, many white stamens and many carpels. These enlarge in fruit to form round heads of achenes, each with a plume-like tail.

Traveller's Joy
Clematis vitalba

Columbine, *Aquilegia vulgaris*, is a perennial plant with a clump of compound leaves and flowering stems 60–90cm (2–3ft) tall in early summer. Each dumpy blue flower has five petal-like sepals with short claws and five petals with long claws containing nectar. The flowers are followed by clusters of pods. Columbines are found in mountain meadows and woods across much of Europe and scattered in wet woods and other wet places through much of the British Isles. They are also grown in gardens.

Columbine
Aquilegia vulgaris

Common Meadow Rue, *Thalictrum flavum*, is one of several *Thalictrum* species in Europe. It is a perennial with a clump of delicate leaves divided into lobed leaflets. The flowers grow in branched inflorescences on stems 1m (3ft) tall; they have petal-like sepals in bud, but these fall as the flowers open, leaving many yellow stamens. Plants grow beside streams and in meadows across Europe and in Great Britain north to Inverness.

Common Meadow Rue
Thalictrum flavum

Meadow Buttercup
Ranunculus acris

Goldilocks
Ranunculus auricomus

Lesser Spearwort
Ranunculus flammula

Buttercup family

There are about 130 species of **Buttercups**, **Crowfoots** and **Spearworts** in Europe, all in the genus *Ranunculus*. They have open, yellow or white flowers, usually with five petals and many carpels which enlarge in fruit to form achenes. All species are acrid.

Meadow Buttercup, *Ranunculus acris*, is a hairy, perennial plant with an erect, branched stem up to 1m (3ft) tall, palmately cut leaves and glossy yellow flowers around midsummer. It grows in damp meadows, on roadsides and near ditches, in gullies and damp ledges in mountain areas throughout the British Isles and much of Europe. Bulbous Buttercup, *R. bulbosus*, is found in similar but drier places. It is like the Meadow Buttercup but comes into flower earlier, has a swollen stem base and reflexed sepals. Creeping Buttercup, *R. repens*, grows in grassy places, damp meadows and woods, and as a weed in gardens, arable land and roadsides throughout Europe and the British Isles. It is a creeping plant with rosettes of long-stalked, three-lobed leaves, eventually making extensive mats, and glossy yellow flowers.

Goldilocks, *Ranunculus auricomus*, grows in woods and hedgerows, mostly in moist, calcareous soils, throughout much of Europe, in Great Britain and Ireland. It is a perennial, with a clump of long-stalked, rounded but deeply lobed leaves. Its flowering stems grow up to 40cm (15in) tall, bear leaves with linear segments and have glossy yellow flowers, some with petals missing.

Lesser Spearwort, *Ranunculus flammula*, is a very acrid species found beside water, in marshes, wet meadows and woods, usually on calcareous soils, throughout Europe and the British Isles. Its prostrate stems root at the nodes and turn upwards to bear linear or lance-shaped leaves and small, clusters of glossy, yellow flowers.

Celery-leaved Crowfoot, *Ranunculus sceleratus*, is the most acrid of all the buttercups, causing blisters if handled. It grows beside water, in marshes and wet meadows throughout Europe, in Great Britain and Ireland. It is an annual, with hollow, hairless stems up to 60cm (2ft) tall and palmately cut leaves, the upper ones with quite narrow segments. The small, pale yellow flowers appear in summer and are followed by cylindrical heads of achenes.

Many *Ranunculus* species are aquatic plants with white flowers. **Common Water-crowfoot**, *R. aquatilis*, is one of the most common of these, growing in slow streams, ponds and ditches throughout Europe and lowland areas of the British Isles, except northwestern Scotland. It has finely dissected, submerged leaves on long, submerged stems, rounded, palmately lobed floating leaves and small white flowers projecting above the surface of the water in early summer.

Lesser Celandine, *Ranunculus ficaria*, is a small perennial plant which forms mats of leaf rosettes in late winter and spring. The leaves are hairless, long-stalked with heart-shaped blades. The flowers are solitary, glossy and bright yellow, fading to white. This plant grows in woods and hedgerows, in damp pastures, beside streams, on damp roadsides and in disturbed places throughout Europe and the British Isles.

Celery-leaved Crowfoot
Ranunculus sceleratus

Common Water-crowfoot
Ranunculus aquatilis

Lesser Celandine
Ranunculus ficaria

Water-lily family

Nymphaeaceae A very small family of
freshwater plants, with about 6 genera
and 70 species, found in many parts of
the world. They are famous for their
beautiful floating leaves and flowers.

   Family features Flowers floating or
projecting out of the water; solitary,
hermaphrodite, regular, often showy.
Sepals 4–6, free; petals numerous
sometimes becoming stamen-like near
the centre of the flower; stamens
numerous; ovary usually superior with 8
carpels. Fruits are capsules. Leaves
floating, round or heart-shaped,
attached by long stalks to rhizomes in
the mud. Some species also have
submerged leaves.

White Water-lily
Nymphaea alba

White Water-lily, *Nymphaea alba*, is
found in ponds and lakes, slow-moving
rivers and canals in lowland areas of the
British Isles and Europe, northwards to
southern Scandinavia. Its floating leaves
are long-stalked with round blades; its
flowers are also floating, fragrant, white
or pink-tinged with yellow stamens. As
the flowers finish, their long stalks coil
and pull them below the surface and the
capsules ripen under water. When they
burst, the seeds rise to the surface.

Yellow Water-lily
Nuphar lutea

Yellow Water-lily *Nuphar lutea*, also
grows in ponds and slow-moving
streams in lowland areas of Europe and
the British Isles, but is rare in Scotland.
It has long-stalked, leathery, heart-
shaped floating leaves and similar, thin
submerged leaves. The bowl-shaped
flowers project above the water; each
has 5–6 thick, yellow sepals and many
similar petals and stamens surrounding
the disk-like stigma. The flowers smell
of alcohol. The fruits are shaped like
brandy bottles and ripen above water.

Fumitory family

Fumariaceae About 16 genera and 450 species, all herbs, found in northern temperate regions and North Africa. Bleeding Heart and Dutchman's Breeches are popular garden plants.

Family features Flowers bilaterally symmetrical, hermaphrodite. Sepals 2, soon falling; petals 4 (2 inner petals often joined together over the stigma, and 2 outer spurred petals, separate at the base but joined at their tips); stamens 6, in 2 groups of 3 with joined filaments, opposite the outer petals; ovary has 1 cell. Fruit is a capsule or nutlet. These are smooth, brittle plants with alternate, divided leaves.

Common Fumitory
Fumaria officinalis

Common Fumitory, *Fumaria officinalis*, is a small, straggling plant with much-divided leaves and loose spikes of flowers. These are tubular, pink with red-tipped spurs. Plants grow in light soils in cultivated ground throughout Europe and the British Isles, most commonly in the east.

Yellow Corydalis
Corydalis lutea

Yellow Corydalis, *Corydalis lutea*, is native to the foothills of the Alps, but has become naturalized in old walls over much of Europe and the British Isles. It forms a clump of branched, brittle stems about 30cm (1ft) tall, with ferny leaves and yellow flowers. These have the typical *Corydalis* form in which only the upper petal is spurred.

Climbing Corydalis, *Corydalis claviculata*, is an annual with branched, climbing stems, pinnate leaves with elliptical segments ending in tendrils and racemes of creamy-white flowers. It grows in woods and shady, rocky places on acid soils, locally in western Europe and over much of the British Isles.

Climbing Corydalis
Corydalis claviculata

Poppy family

Papaveraceae About 26 genera and 200 species, mostly herbs with a few shrubs and trees, found mainly in subtropical and temperate regions of the northern hemisphere. Some are grown in gardens.

Family features Flowers usually solitary, regular, hermaphrodite. Sepals 2–3, soon falling; petals 4–6 or 8–12, free, often crumpled; stamens many; ovary superior with 2 or more united carpels. Fruits are capsules, opening by pores or valves. Leaves alternate and often much divided. Stipules 0. The plants contain coloured sap.

The **Field Poppy**, *Papaver rhoeas*, is the one which grew on Flanders fields after the First World War, becoming the symbol of Remembrance Day. At one time it was a common cornfield weed, but now more often grows on roadsides and in waste places, usually on calcareous soils. It is found throughout Europe and much of the British Isles. It is a stiffly hairy, annual plant with an erect stem up to 60cm (2ft) tall, divided leaves and red, four-petalled, bowl-shaped flowers opening from nodding buds. At the centre of each flower is a ring of black anthers encircling a round stigma. The capsules resemble pepper pots, each with a ring of holes around the rim, scattering their tiny seeds as they sway in the wind. Prickly Long-headed Poppy, *P. argemone*, is similar but has bristly hairs on stems, sepals and capsules.

Probably the most famous member of the family is the **Opium Poppy**, *Papaver somniferum*, whose capsules provide opium, source of morphine and heroin. Poppy seeds are rich in oil

Field Poppy
Papaver rhoeas

Opium Poppy
Papaver somniferum

which is used in soaps, paints, salad oils and cattle cake. Opium Poppies are probably native to the Mediterranean but grow as casual weeds in cultivated land and waste places elsewhere in Europe and in Britain. They are annual, more or less hairless plants up to 1.5m (5ft) tall, with pinnately lobed or toothed leaves and large, pale purple flowers, often with black blotches.

Welsh Poppy, *Meconopsis cambrica*, is a perennial with a clump of pinnately lobed, basal leaves. In early summer it produces erect, leafy flowering stems 30–60cm (1–2ft) tall, with solitary yellow flowers on long stalks. Plants grow in damp, shady places, beside walls and among rocks in Wales and southwest England, in the Massif Central in France and in northern Spain. Elsewhere they are grown in, and escape from, gardens.

Yellow Horned-poppy, *Glaucium flavum*, grows on the west and south coasts of Britain and the west coast of Europe, on shingle banks, sand-dunes, cliffs and waste land. It is a perennial, somewhat fleshy, grey-blue plant, with a branched stem 30–90cm (1–3ft) tall and pinnately lobed leaves. In summer its yellow flowers are followed by long, sickle-shaped capsules.

Greater Celandine, *Chelidonium majus*, is a former herbal plant with caustic orange sap used to treat warts. It grows in hedgerows or beneath walls, usually near dwellings, throughout most of Europe and in lowland areas of Great Britain and Ireland. It is a perennial up to 1m (3ft) tall, with almost hairless divided leaves on erect, brittle stems. The small, pale yellow flowers are followed by slender capsules.

Welsh Poppy
Meconopsis cambrica

Yellow Horned-poppy
Glaucium flavum

Greater Celandine
Chelidonium majus

Mustard family

Cruciferae or Brassicaceae. An important family with about 375 genera and 3200 species of herbs found mainly in north temperate regions. It contains many crop plants, including cabbages, mustard and rape, garden plants like aubrietas, alyssum and wallflowers, and many weeds.

Family features Flowers in racemes, regular, hermaphrodite. Sepals 4, free; petals 4, free, in the form of a cross; stamens 6; ovary superior. Fruits are specialized capsules (siliquas) with 2 valves opening from below, exposing a central septum to which seeds are attached. Leaves alternate. Stipules 0.

The genus *Brassica* is one that has produced many important crop plants. *Brassica oleracea* has produced cabbages, cauliflowers, broccoli, Brussels sprouts and kale; *B. rapa* is the turnip; *B. napus* has produced rape and swede; *B. nigra* is Black Mustard.

Wild Cabbage, *Brassica oleracea*, is a maritime plant in its wild state, growing on cliffs on the coasts of France, Spain and Italy, southern England and Wales. This is a biennial or perennial plant, with a strong tap root and a thick, sprawling stem. The leaves are grey and cabbage-like, pinnately lobed or with wavy edges. The flowers are borne in an erect inflorescence in summer and are followed by cylindrical, beaked fruits.

Charlock, *Sinapis arvensis*, was at one time a serious weed of vegetable and grain crops, but has become less so with the advent of modern weedkillers; it still grows in arable land, around the edges of fields and in waste places, especially where the soil is heavy or calcareous,

Wild Cabbage
Brassica oleracea

Charlock
Sinapis arvensis

throughout Europe, Great Britain and Ireland. This annual plant has a stiffly hairy, erect stem and roughly hairy leaves, becoming simpler higher up the stem. The bright yellow flowers produce long-beaked pods held upright and containing dark red-brown seeds. They can be used as a substitute for those of Black Mustard.

Wild Radish, *Raphanus raphanistrum*, is another pernicious weed found throughout Europe, Great Britain and Ireland, especially on calcareous soils. This annual plant has rough, hairy stems, lobed leaves and yellowish, mauve-veined flowers. The long, cylindrical fruits become ribbed and constricted between each seed as they dry out, eventually breaking up into single-seeded sections.

Wild Radish
Raphanus raphanistrum

Like Wild Cabbage, **Seakale**, *Crambe maritima*, is a maritime plant growing on shingle banks and sandy beaches, or on cliffs and among rocks along the Baltic and Atlantic coasts of Europe, including those of Britain and Ireland. It is a perennial, with a fleshy crown and large clumps of blue-green, pinnately lobed leaves. In summer the plant bears broad clusters of white flowers followed by rounded fruits.

Seakale
Crambe maritima

Sea Rocket, *Cakile maritima*, grows on drift lines on shingle banks and sandy beaches around the coasts of Europe and the British Isles. It is an annual with sprawling, branched stems radiating from a central tap root. The stems are leafy, with succulent, greyish leaves, varying in shape from pinnately lobed to entire. Purple flowers appear around midsummer in dense, terminal inflorescences; they are followed by stubby fruits.

Sea Rocket
Cakile maritima

Mustard family

Field Pepperwort
Lepidium campestre

The **Pepperworts** are members of the genus *Lepidium*, a variable group of annual to perennial plants, all with dense racemes of white flowers. There are 21 species in Europe. **Field Pepperwort**, *L. campestre*, is an annual, grey-green plant with a branched, erect stem up to 60cm (2ft) tall, lyre-shaped basal leaves and triangular stem leaves, their bases clasping the stem. Its tiny white flowers are followed by rounded, notched fruits, white-scaly when mature. Plants grow in dry, grassy places, on roadsides and banks, in arable land and on walls throughout Europe and Great Britain; it is rare in Scotland and Ireland. The young shoots may be eaten in salads. Smith's Cress, *L. heterophyllum*, is similar but smaller and perennial, and its fruits lack scales.

Swine-cress
Coronopus squamatus

Swine-cress, *Coronopus squamatus*, is a small annual or biennial plant with branched, prostrate stems and pinnately lobed leaves. The small white flowers grow in dense clusters in the leaf axils in summer and are followed by large, kidney-shaped, warty fruits, usually the first thing to catch the eye. This little plant grows in waste places, often on bare ground, throughout southern England, becoming rarer in the north, also in Ireland and throughout Europe. Lesser Swine-cress, *C. didymus,* has pitted fruits and a sulphurous smell.

Hoary Cress
Cardaria draba

Hoary Cress, *Cardaria draba*, is a serious weed. It is a perennial plant which forms a spreading colony with roots which may penetrate to a depth of 3m (10ft), so once established it becomes very difficult to eradicate. It is found in many parts of Europe, including much of Great Britain (most commonly in the south), and is scattered through Ireland. It grows in cultivated land, on roadsides and railway embankments and in other disturbed places. Each shoot grows to about 90cm (3ft) tall, has hairy, deeply toothed leaves, those on the stem with clasping bases, and dense, umbel-like clusters of white flowers borne on long stalks in the upper leaf axils in early summer. The fruits are kidney-shaped and split into single-seeded sections.

Field
Pennycress
Thlaspi arvense

Field Pennycress, *Thlaspi arvense* is an annual plant with a foetid scent. It has an erect stem 60cm (2ft) tall, with clasping, lance-shaped leaves and a cluster of small white flowers which gradually give way to broadly winged, flattened fruits, each one notched at the top. The plant grows in waste places and cultivated land throughout Europe and the British Isles; it can be a serious weed if allowed to seed.

Shepherd's Purse, *Capsella bursa-pastoris*, is a familiar garden weed found throughout the world. It is a small annual or biennial plant with a basal rosette of simple, more or less lobed leaves and an erect flowering stem up to 40cm (15in) tall. The flowers are white and very small, borne in an elongating inflorescence and followed by heart-shaped capsules, like little purses.

Shepherd's Purse
Capsella bursa-pastoris

Shepherd's Cress, *Teesdalia nudicaulis*, grows in sandy and gravelly places throughout much of Europe and Great Britain, but it is rare in Scotland and Ireland. This is another small annual plant, with a rosette of pinnately divided leaves and elongating racemes of white flowers followed by ovate, narrowly winged fruits.

Shepherd's Cress
Teesdalia nudicaulis

Mustard family

Common Scurvy-grass, *Cochlearia officinalis*, is one of several Scurvy-grasses which grow on coasts around Europe and the British Isles. This one grows mostly in salt marshes but also on grassy banks, cliffs and shingle. At one time plants were collected for the Vitamin C found in their leaves but oranges taste much better. Common Scurvy-grass is a biennial or perennial plant growing up to 60cm (2ft) tall, with a rosette of fleshy, long-stalked, heart-shaped leaves and sprawling, leafy flowering stems. The many white flowers are borne in early summer in branched inflorescences. They are followed by globular fruits.

Common Scurvy-grass
Cochlearia officinalis

Woad, *Isatis tinctoria*, was at one time cultivated in many areas of Britain and Europe for the blue dye which can be extracted from it. However, it has now largely been replaced by indigo and has become very rare in Britain, even though it is still found in waste places and fields in other parts of Europe. It usually grows as a biennial, with several rosettes of softly hairy, lance-shaped basal leaves and erect, leafy flowering stems growing up to 120cm (4ft) tall. The stems branch near the top to form many dense racemes of yellow flowers which are followed by purple-brown, drooping, flattened fruits.

Common Whitlow Grass, *Erophila verna*, is an annual plant with a small clump of hairy, spoon-shaped leaves and a flowering stem only 20cm (8in) tall at most, much smaller in poor conditions. Its minute flowers are white with deeply notched petals and they are followed by little elliptical pods. Common Whitlow Grass grows on walls and among rocks,

Woad
Isatis tinctoria

in grassy places and dry banks, on arable land and roadsides, usually on calcareous or neutral soils, throughout the British Isles and Europe, north to central Norway.

Horse Radish, *Armoracia rusticana*, probably came originally from southeastern Europe but is grown in many parts of the Continent, as well as England and Wales. Its roots are used to make horseradish sauce. It has escaped in many countries to grow wild in fields and waste places, on roadsides and beside streams, especially near dwellings and in lowland areas. It forms wide colonies with many leaf rosettes, each rosette at the top of a long, fleshy tap root. The leaves are large and oblong, toothed and long-stalked. In early summer plants may produce erect flowering stems up to 120cm (4ft) tall, with spreading inflorescences and many white flowers followed by globular fruits. However, northern plants often do not flower, and if they do, the seeds may not ripen.

Wintercress, *Barbarea vulgaris*, is another edible crucifer. Its rosettes of leaves, appearing in late winter, are an excellent addition to salads, rich in Vitamin C and with a taste like watercress. The leaves may also be eaten as a green vegetable like spinach, and the early flower buds are like broccoli. In summer the rosettes produce erect, branched, leafy stems 30–90cm (1–3ft) tall, with inflorescences of bright yellow flowers. These are followed by long, straight fruits held erect. This plant grows on damp roadsides and beside ditches, in hedgerows and on stream banks throughout Great Britain and Ireland, and in much of Europe.

Common
Whitlow
Grass
Erophila verna

Horse Radish
*Armoracia
rusticana*

Wintercress
Barbarea vulgaris

Cuckoo-flower
Cardamine pratensis

Mustard family

The **Bittercresses**, belonging to the
genus *Cardamine*, consist of a group of
about 120 species found throughout the
world, with over 35 in Europe.
Cuckoo-flower or Lady's Smock,
Cardamine pratensis, grows in wet
meadows and marshes, beside ponds
and streams, in open woods and other
damp, grassy places throughout the
British Isles and Europe. It forms
rosettes of pinnate leaves with ovate
leaflets, and in late spring produces
delicate, lilac-pink flowers on an erect
stem about 60cm (2ft) tall. The petals
are notched and the fruits which follow
are elongated and flattened.

Hairy Bittercress, *Cardamine hirsuta*,
is an annual plant, also with rosettes of
pinnate leaves, but the leaf segments in
this plant are lobed or angled and
sparsely hairy. It forms erect, leafy
stems up to 30cm (1ft) tall, with
terminal racemes of small, white flowers
followed by long, thin fruits. These
open explosively on touch, catapulting
out their seeds (a characteristic of all
Cardamine species). Hairy Bittercress
grows as a weed on cultivated and bare
ground (where it may be only 5cm (2in)
tall), on walls and rocks throughout
Europe and the British Isles.

The **Rockcresses** in the genus *Arabis*
are a large group of some 120 species
found throughout temperate regions of
the northern hemisphere, with about 35
in Europe. White Arabis, *A. albida*, is a
well-known rock garden plant. **Hairy
Rockcress**, *A. hirsuta*, is a short-lived
perennial or biennial plant with a
rosette of simple basal leaves, an erect,
leafy flowering stem and white flowers
followed by cylindrical fruits held erect.

Hairy Bittercress
Cardamine hirsuta

It grows on walls and limestone rocks, dry banks and dunes throughout the British Isles and most of Europe. Tower Mustard, *A. glabra*, is an overwintering annual or biennial plant with a rosette of linear, toothed leaves which wither before the flowers appear. The erect flowering stem grows up to 120cm (4ft) tall, with arrow-like leaves and pale yellow flowers followed by long, slender pods. Plants grow on dry banks and cliffs, roadsides and waste places, in open woods and heaths throughout much of Europe, locally in England.

Hairy Rockcress
Arabis hirsuta

Watercress, *Nasturtium officinale*, has a distinctive biting taste and is eaten in salads; it is rich in Vitamins A and C. The cultivated form is like the wild form, which grows in quiet streams and springs throughout lowland areas of the British Isles and Europe, north to southern Scandinavia. This is a dark green plant with hollow stems which root in the mud and then grow up to float on the surface. It has compound leaves with 5−9 leaflets. The racemes of white flowers appear in summer and are followed by erect, curving, cylindrical fruits.

Watercress
Nasturtium officinale

The **Yellowcresses**, belonging to the genus *Rorippa*, are a large group of species related to Watercress but inedible and with yellow flowers. Many grow in wet places or beside streams and ditches. **Marsh Yellowcress**, *R. palustris*, is an annual or biennial plant with a rosette of sinuately lobed leaves and an erect, leafy flowering stem in summer. The flowers are pale yellow and followed by egg-shaped fruits. This plant grows most often on bare ground where water stands in winter; it is found in much of Europe and lowland areas of the British Isles.

Marsh Yellowcress
Rorippa palustris

Mustard family

Treacle Mustard, *Erysimum cheiranthoides*, is a weed of waste places, roadsides and cultivated land across most of Europe, mainly in southern England in the British Isles. It is rare in the north, in Scotland, Wales and Ireland. It is a hairy annual plant, with a rosette of irregularly toothed leaves withering before flowering, and branched, leafy stems up to 90cm (3ft) tall in summer. These bear flat-topped clusters of buds and bright yellow flowers above a lengthening array of long, curved fruits. This is an old herbal plant often known as Wormseed, since its seeds were a potent but dangerous remedy for worms.

Treacle Mustard
Erysimum cheiranthoides

Garlic Mustard or Jack-by-the-hedge, *Alliaria petiolata*, is most often found at the base of a hedgerow or on roadsides, in woods, gardens, farmyards and waste places throughout Europe and the British Isles. Its leaves smell of garlic when bruised and can be used in sauces as a substitute for garlic, or eaten in salads. This is a biennial plant, with a rosette of long-stalked, dark green, kidney-shaped, toothed leaves in the first year and a leafy flowering stem about 1m (3ft) tall in the second. This ends in a lengthening inflorescence of white flowers borne in late spring and early summer. The fruits are long, cylindrical and curved.

There are many *Sisymbrium* species in Europe and Asia, many of them weeds of waste places, roadsides and cultivated land. They characteristically have yellow flowers and long, beakless fruits which contain one row of small seeds. **Hedge Mustard**, *S. officinale*, can be recognized from the way the flowering

Garlic Mustard
Alliaria petiolata

stems jut out from the main branches, almost at right angles; when in fruit these stems become very elongated, with long, overlapping fruits pressed closely against the stems. This is an annual, unbranched roughly bristly plant about 60cm (2ft) tall, with deeply cut basal leaves and narrow, toothed stem leaves. The small, pale yellow flowers appear over a long period during the summer, soon forming a small cluster over an elongating array of fruits. Plants grow in hedgebanks and on roadsides, in waste and cultivated land throughout Europe and the British Isles, much less commonly in northern Scotland.

Hedge Mustard
Sisymbrium officinale

Thale Cress, *Arabidopsis thaliana*, is another weedy species, found on walls and banks, in hedgerows and waste places, especially in sandy soils, throughout the British Isles and Europe. It is an annual plant, with a rosette of greyish-green, spoon-shaped or elliptical, often toothed leaves, and erect stems up to 50cm (20in) tall. The stems have similar, usually untoothed, leaves and inflorescences of small white flowers followed by long, linear fruits.

Thale Cress
Arabidopsis thaliana

Gold-of-pleasure, *Camelina sativa*, is now a casual plant in Britain where once it was a common weed of cultivated land, often growing with flax; its numbers have declined with modern farming techniques. It is scattered across much of Europe, introduced from the east and at one time was widely cultivated for the fibres in its stems and the oil extracted from its seeds. This is an annual plant with erect stems up to 1m (3ft) tall and arrow-shaped leaves with bases clasping the stems. The golden yellow flowers grow in an elongating inflorescence and are followed by woody, pear-shaped fruits.

Gold-of-pleasure
Camelina sativa

Dyer's Rocket
Reseda luteola

Wild Mignonette
Reseda lutea

Mignonette family

Resedaceae Only 6 genera but 700 species of herbs found mainly in the Mediterranean region. Mignonette is grown for its fragrant flowers.

Family features Flowers borne in spike-like racemes; irregular, hermaphrodite. Sepals 4–7, fused into a tube; petals 4–7, those at the back larger and more deeply divided than those at the front of the flower; stamens numerous, crowded to the front of the flower; ovary superior, with 2–6 cells joined at the base. Fruit a capsule. Leaves alternate, simple or pinnately divided, with small, gland-like stipules.

For centuries **Dyer's Rocket**, *Reseda luteola*, was cultivated as a source of yellow dye used to colour wool and other fabrics, until it was replaced by modern synthetic dyes. Today it grows in waste places, beside roads, on old walls, sand-dunes and dry banks, most often on calcareous soils, locally in Europe north to southern Scandinavia, in Great Britain and Ireland. It is a biennial plant with a rosette of narrow, lance-shaped leaves in the first year and an erect flowering stem up to 1.5m (5ft) tall in the second. The stem has many narrow leaves and a slender spike of yellow-green flowers. Each flower has four sepals and four petals, the front petal linear, back and side petals divided into several lobes.

Wild Mignonette, *Reseda lutea*, is only 60cm (2ft) tall and often perennial with many branched stems. Its pinnately divided leaves are distinctive for their lobes are blunt and diverge widely from the narrow, central portion of the leaf, which is constricted above each lobe. The flowers are borne in conical racemes; each one has six petals, back and side petals divided and the front two linear. Plants grow in calcareous soils, on dry banks and roadsides, in quarries and waste places, in cultivated land and chalk downs. They are found in western Europe and the Mediterranean region, throughout England and Wales, locally in Scotland and Ireland.

Sundew family

Droseraceae These are insectivorous plants with rosettes of sticky, glandular leaves which function as insect traps. They have regular flowers, usually with 5 separate sepals and petals, 5 stamens and a single ovary. There are 4 genera and about 105 species, found throughout the world in acid soils, in sandy and boggy places.

Round-leaved Sundew, *Drosera rotundifolia*, grows in bogs and wet, peaty places on moors and heaths throughout Europe and the British Isles. This tiny plant has a flat rosette of long-stalked leaves, their round blades covered in red-tipped glands which secrete a sticky fluid. Insects are trapped and digested on the leaves and the nutrients absorbed. In summer the plants produce leafless flowering stems about 20cm (8in) tall, with one-sided clusters of small white or pink flowers.

Round-leaved Sundew
Drosera rotundifolia

Great Sundew, *Drosera anglica*, likes the wettest parts of bogs, growing among *Sphagnum* mosses. In the British Isles it is most common in Ireland, northwest Scotland and other wet areas, and is also found in northern Europe. Its leaves are held more or less erect, have long stalks and elongated blades with glandular, red-tipped hair.

Great Sundew
Drosera anglica

Biting Stonecrop
Sedum acre

White Stonecrop
Sedum album

Orpine
Sedum telephium

Stonecrop family

Crassulaceae About 35 genera and 1500 species of herbs and small shrubs, mostly found in dry, warm temperate regions of the world. Some are grown in rock gardens, others as house plants.

Family features Flowers often star-like and borne in cymes; regular, hermaphrodite. Sepals and petals 4 or 5, free or united; stamens as many as and alternating with petals, or twice as many; ovary superior with as many carpels as petals, free or united at the base. Fruits membranous or leathery pods. Many members of this family are succulent. Leaves in dense rosettes, opposite or alternate. Stipules 0.

Stonecrops form a large group of about 600 species in the genus *Sedum*, mostly found in the northern hemisphere. Nearly 60 grow wild in Europe, and more are grown in gardens. They are succulent plants, many small and mat-like in form, with prostrate stems and leaves in rosettes. They often grow in the poorest of soils or clinging to rocks, like **Biting Stonecrop**, *S. acre*. This little plant has mats of prostrate stems and bright green, often red-tinged leaves transformed by bright yellow flowers in summer. The flowers grow in clusters at the tops of erect stems, only 10cm (4in) tall at most. Plants grow on walls and rocky banks, in dry grassland, on dunes and shingle, often in calcareous soils, throughout the British Isles and Europe.

White Stonecrop, *Sedum album*, is a similar but more straggly plant with creeping stems and upright flowering stems; both have bright green, sometimes red-tinged leaves. The flowering stems grow 15cm (6in) tall and have clusters of white flowers. This plant grows wild on rocks and walls across much of Europe and the British Isles, probably as an escape from gardens in many places.

Other stonecrops are larger plants with clumps of upright, leafy stems. **Orpine**, *Sedum telephium*, is grown in gardens and also grows wild in woods and hedgebanks throughout much of Europe and the British Isles, often in sandy soils. It is a grey-green, often red-tinged perennial plant, its stems 20–60cm (8in–2ft) tall, with alternate, toothed leaves. In late summer they bear dense clusters of red-purple flowers in the axils of the upper leaves.

Houseleek, *Sempervivum tectorum*, is one of about 25 *Sempervivum* species found in the mountains of Europe and often grown in rock gardens. Houseleek is grown on roofs in many parts of Europe to protect the house from fire and lightning, according to folklore. It forms rosettes of pointed, blue-green, red-tipped leaves, each rosette up to 8cm (3in) across, spreading into patches with new rosettes. Each year some rosettes in the patch flower and then die; they produce erect, leafy stems 30–60cm (1–2ft) tall tipped with a flat cluster of spiky-looking, pink flowers.

Wall Pennywort, *Umbilicus rupestris*, forms clumps of thick, rounded leaves, each with a dimple in the centre where the stalk joins at the back. In summer plants produce erect flowering stems with long racemes of bell-shaped, greenish-white flowers. They grow in walls and banks, especially on acid soils, in western and Mediterranean Europe, Ireland and western areas of Britain, north to southern Scotland.

Houseleek
Sempervivum tectorum

Wall Pennywort
Umbilicus rupestris

Purple Saxifrage
Saxifraga oppositifolia

Saxifrage family

Saxifragaceae About 30 genera and 580 species of herbs, mainly from temperate regions of the northern hemisphere. Many species are grown in rock gardens and flower borders.

Family features Flowers usually regular and hermaphrodite. Sepals and petals 5, alternating (in some species petals 0); stamens 5–10; ovary has 2 carpels often joined together at the base. The flowers have a flat ring around the ovary, often glistening with nectar, on which stamens, petals and sepals are inserted. Fruits are capsules. Leaves alternate. Stipules 0.

The **Saxifrages**, belonging to the genus *Saxifraga*, are much the largest group in the family with over 300 species, many growing in the high mountains like the Alps and Caucasus, others at lower altitudes in woods and meadows.

Purple Saxifrage, *Saxifraga oppositifolia*, forms loose mats of stems with opposite, fleshy leaves, so close together at the tips that they look like rosettes. This is a very small plant, growing 8–10cm (3–4in) high at most; its solitary purple flowers are borne at the tips of the stems in late summer. It grows in limestone soils, among rock debris and on slopes in the mountains of Europe and the British Isles.

Meadow Saxifrage
Saxifraga granulata

Meadow Saxifrage, *Saxifraga granulata*, is a much more widespread plant growing in grassland, usually on well-drained neutral or alkaline soils, throughout most of Europe. In Britain it is more common in the east, absent from southwestern England and northern Scotland, rare in Ireland. It forms a clump of hairy, lobed, kidney-

Mossy Saxifrage
Saxifraga hypnoides

shaped leaves with long stalks, appearing in spring and dying down soon after the white flowers bloom in early summer. A double form is grown in gardens.

Mossy Saxifrage, *Saxifraga hypnoides*, is a wild form of the mossy saxifrages grown in gardens. It grows on ledges and screes, in damp, grassy places and beside streams in the mountains and hills of northwestern Europe and in suitable places throughout much of Great Britain and Ireland. It forms a mat of leafy shoots and flowering rosettes, with white flowers in early summer borne in clusters on erect stalks.

Opposite-leaved Golden Saxifrage, *Chrysosplenium oppositifolium*, grows in shady, wet places, beside springs and streams in western and central Europe, and throughout much of the British Isles, more commonly in the west. It often spreads into wide patches with its creeping, leafy stems. The leaves are opposite, rounded or kidney-shaped with wavy edges and long stalks. In summer the stems turn upwards to bloom, producing tiny, yellow-green flowers surrounded by bright yellow-green bracts. The flowers lack petals.

Opposite-leaved
Golden Saxifrage
*Chrysosplenium
oppositifolium*

Grass of Parnassus, *Parnassia palustris*, grows beside streams and lakes, in wet meadows, bogs and marshes across most of Europe, locally in Great Britain and Ireland where its numbers are declining. This perennial plant has a rosette of long-stalked, heart-shaped leaves and solitary white flowers on erect flowering stalks. It can be identified by the pattern of the stamens in the flower — five fertile stamens between the petals and five fringed sterile ones opposite the petals.

Grass of Parnassus
Parnassia palustris

Rose family

Rosaceae A large and important
family, with about 100 genera and over
2000 species, found throughout the
world, especially in temperate regions.
The family includes fruit trees, like
apple, pear and cherry, together with
many ornamental shrubs, trees and
herbs for the garden.

Family features Flowers regular,
hermaphrodite; sepals and petals 5, free,
often overlapping; stamens numerous;
ovary superior with the floral parts in
rings around its base, or inferior; ovary
has one to many carpels, free or united;
the styles usually remain free. Fruits are
achenes, drupes or pomes. Leaves
simple or compound, usually alternate,
generally with 2 stipules.

Meadowsweet
Filipendula ulmaria

Dropwort
Filipendula vulgaris

Meadowsweet, *Filipendula ulmaria*,
grows throughout Europe and the
British Isles, often in abundance in wet
woods, meadows and marshes, and on
riverbanks. It is a perennial plant with
clumps of dark green, pinnate leaves
and erect, leafy flowering stems,
60–120cm (2–4ft) tall, in summer.
Each leaf has up to five pairs of large
leaflets with smaller leaflets in between.
The flowers are small with creamy-
white petals and long stamens, sweetly
scented and borne in clusters. The
fruits consist of several carpels which
become twisted around each other so
that they look like spirals.

Dropwort, *Filipendula vulgaris*, grows
in calcareous grassland, often on downs
and limestone uplands, throughout
much of Europe north to southern
Norway, and in England. This
perennial plant forms clumps of pinnate
leaves with many toothed leaflets, larger
leaflets alternating with smaller ones. In

summer the almost leafless flowering stems grow up to 80cm (30in) tall, each tipped with a flat-topped cluster of creamy-white flowers opening from pink buds. The fruits are hairy and the carpels are not twisted together.

Water Avens, *Geum rivale*, grows in wet meadows and marshes, in wet woods and beside streams across much of Europe and the British Isles. It forms a clump of compound, pinnate leaves, each one with a very broad terminal leaflet. The flowers are borne in loose clusters on leafy flowering stems; they are nodding with purplish sepals and orange-pink petals. The centre of each flower, like those of all avens, contains many carpels which enlarge into achenes. In this species the long styles become hooked and the fruits become burs which catch in fur or clothing.

Water Avens
Geum rivale

Wood Avens, *Geum urbanum*, is a perennial plant with a clump of hairy, compound leaves; each leaf has 2–3 pairs of lateral leaflets and one large, lobed terminal leaflet. In early summer the small yellow flowers appear in loose clusters on separate leafy stalks 20–60cm (8in-2ft) tall. The fruits form burs with jointed hooks. Plants grow in shady, damp places in woods and hedgerows throughout Europe and the British Isles, except the extreme north.

Wood Avens
Geum urbanum

White Mountain Avens, *Dryas octopetala*, grows on ledges in the mountains of Europe, Scotland, Ireland and northern England, rarely in Wales. It is also grown in rock gardens. It has prostrate, semi-woody stems and leaves like miniature oak leaves. The white flowers grow on erect stalks in early summer, followed by plumed achenes with white feathery styles.

White Mountain Avens
Dryas octopetala

Rose family

The **Cinquefoils**, members of the genus *Potentilla*, are a large group of mostly perennial plants, with over 75 species in Europe. Their flowers have 5 petals cupped not only in green sepals but also in an epicalyx — this looks like a second set of sepals. Many have yellow flowers and their fruits are clusters of dry achenes, often partly enclosed by the persistent calyx.

Creeping Cinquefoil
Potentilla reptans

Creeping Cinquefoil, *Potentilla reptans*, has leaves typical of many cinquefoils; they are long-stalked and palmately compound, with several toothed leaflets (often five, hence cinquefoil). It has prostrate stems, rosettes of long-stalked leaves and solitary, bright yellow flowers in summer. This plant is common on roadside verges, in waste places and hedgebanks, less often in grassland, mostly on basic and neutral soils, throughout the British Isles and much of Europe.

Tormentil
Potentilla erecta

Tormentil, *Potentilla erecta*, grows in acid grassland, on heaths, moors, marshes and in open woods throughout Europe and the British Isles. It has trailing, leafy flowering stems often only 10cm (4in) long; the palmate leaves usually have three leaflets but often appear to have five — the two extras are the stipules. Its flowers distinguish this from other cinquefoils for they have only four petals.

Silverweed
Potentilla anserina

Silverweed, *Potentilla anserina*, grows in moist meadows, damp roadsides, open woods, waste places and sand-dunes across much of Europe and throughout the British Isles. This is a creeping plant with prostrate stems

Barren Strawberry
Potentilla sterilis

rooting at the nodes. Its pinnate leaves have pairs of small, toothed leaflets alternating with larger ones; they are dark green above and silver-hairy beneath. The flowers are the usual cinquefoil ones with yellow petals. Silverweed roots are edible, like parsnips in flavour, but are very small.

Barren Strawberry, *Potentilla sterilis*, looks like a Wild Strawberry but its fruits are small, dry clusters of achenes instead of strawberries. The plant forms small rosettes of long-stalked leaves, each with three leaflets, and has sprawling flowering stems with clusters of white flowers in the leaf axils. It grows in hedgebanks and open woods, in grassy places and roadside verges, usually on dry soils, in western and central Europe, and throughout the British Isles.

Marsh Cinquefoil
Potentilla palustris

Marsh Cinquefoil, *Potentilla palustris*, grows in wet meadows and marshes, wet heaths and moors throughout much of Europe and the British Isles. It has leafy stems 15–45cm (6–18in) tall, with palmately lobed leaves and clusters of flowers in early summer. The flowers are unusual for potentillas — reddish-purple with large, purplish sepals and smaller, darker petals.

Wild Strawberry, *Fragaria vesca*, is a small perennial plant found in woods, grassy places and hedgebanks, usually in base-rich soils, throughout Europe and the British Isles. It forms rosettes of compound leaves (each leaf with three leaflets) and spreads by runners — stems which grow from the mother plant to form new plants. White flowers, and then strawberries, grow in clusters on leafless stalks — the fruits are very small but much sweeter than cultivated ones.

Wild Strawberry
Fragaria vesca

Rose family

Agrimony, *Agrimonia eupatoria*, grows in open woods and hedgebanks, on roadsides and in field margins throughout Europe and much of the British Isles. It forms an erect, leafy stem 30–60cm (1–2ft) tall, with dark green, compound leaves in which large leaflets are interspersed with small ones; the leaflets have toothed margins. In late summer a spike of small yellow flowers forms at the top of the stem. The fruits are distinctive -- top-shaped, with rows of hooked bristles on the top surface; they are dispersed when they get caught in the hair of passing animals.

Agrimony
Agrimonia eupatoria

Great Burnet
Sanguisorba officinalis

Great Burnet, *Sanguisorba officinalis*, is an old herbal plant found in damp grassland throughout much of Europe, most commonly in England and Wales in Britain, declining in numbers in recent years. This is a hairless perennial plant with a rosette of pinnate leaves; each leaf has 3–7 pairs of long-stalked, toothed leaflets, becoming larger towards the tip. In summer the leafy flowering stems appear, 30–90cm (1–3ft) tall, with dense oblong heads of reddish flowers terminating the branches. The colour comes from the sepals for the flowers lack petals.

Salad Burnet, *Sanguisorba minor*, is a smaller plant found in calcareous grassland, usually on chalk and limestone uplands across much of Europe. In Britain it is most common in England and Wales, occurring much more locally in Scotland and Ireland. It forms small, perennial clumps of pinnate leaves, each with 4–12 pairs of toothed leaflets. In summer the flowering stems grow about 60cm (2ft) tall, with pinnate leaves near the base

and rounded flower heads at the top.
Unlike the heads of Great Burnet, in
which the flowers are hermaphrodite,
those of Salad Burnet vary, female
flowers with reddish styles at the top of
each head, hermaphrodite ones in the
centre and hermaphrodite or male
flowers at the base. This plant has a
scent of cucumber when bruised and the
leaves can be added to summer punch.

Lady's Mantles belong to the large
genus *Alchemilla*, with probably over
100 species in Europe. They are
perennial plants with palmate or
palmately lobed leaves and numerous
flowers in branched cymes. The flowers
are green or yellow-green, the colour
coming from the four fused sepals and
epicalyx, for they lack petals. **Common
Lady's Mantle**, *A. vulgaris*, grows in
damp grassland and woods, on stream
banks and rocky ledges, especially on
basic soils, throughout most of Europe
and the British Isles, rarely in
southeastern England. It forms large
clumps of attractive, palmately lobed
leaves that hold drops of water after
rain. The yellow-green flowers are
borne in large, branched clusters on
leafy stalks in summer.

Parsley Piert, *Aphanes arvensis*, grows
on bare ground in arable land, gardens,
waste places and roadsides, also in
grassland and heaths, throughout much
of Europe and the British Isles. This is
a very small, pale green annual plant,
often only 2cm (1in) tall. It has
branched, sprawling stems covered with
fringed, cup-like stipules and fan-
shaped, lobed leaves, each lobe further
divided into three sections. The flowers
are tiny and petal-less, borne in dense
clusters opposite the leaves, each cluster
half cupped in a leafy stipule.

Salad Burnet
Sanguisorba minor

Common Lady's Mantle
Alchemilla vulgaris

Parsley Piert
Aphanes arvensis

Rose family

About 45 Wild Roses, *Rosa* species, grow in Europe. One of the most familiar is the **Dog Rose**, *R. canina*, its arching, prickly branches growing in hedges and woodland margins throughout the British Isles and Europe, except the north. It has stout stems up to 3m (10ft) tall, pinnate leaves with 2–3 pairs of oval, toothed leaflets, stout, curved prickles, and pink or white flowers in summer followed by hairless, elliptical hips. The Field Rose, *R. arvensis*, has weaker, trailing, often purplish stems and white flowers with fused styles.

Sweetbriar or Eglantine, *Rosa rubiginosa*, is usually found on chalk downs or limestone uplands, also on the coast in rough grassland and scrub, throughout most of Europe and much of the British Isles. It is a dense shrub with stout, arching stems 2–3m (6–9ft) tall armed with unequal, flattened, broad-based thorns. The leaves are sticky with red-brown, stalked glands and smell of green apples when crushed. The fragrant, bright pink flowers appear in early summer and are followed by elongated hips.

Burnet Rose, *Rosa pimpinellifolia*, grows on the coasts of Europe, Scotland and Ireland in dune slacks and fixed sand-dunes. It forms dense thickets of erect, extremely prickly stems growing up to 60cm (2ft) tall and covered with numerous straight prickles and many stiff bristles. They bear small, hairless leaves, each with 7–11 rounded, serrated leaflets, and solitary, creamy-white flowers in early summer. The flowers are followed by small rounded hips, turning purplish-black when ripe.

Dog Rose
Rosa canina

Sweetbriar
Rosa rubiginosa

Burnet Rose
Rosa pimpinellifolia

The large group of over 250 *Rubus* species grow mainly in temperate regions of the northern hemisphere. Many are shrubby, perennial plants that nevertheless have a biennial growth pattern. Each year new shoots grow from the base of the plant; these first-year shoots are unbranched, have compound leaves and do not flower. In the second year they produce leafy side branches with flowers and fruits, and then they die.

Blackberry
Rubus fruticosus

The stems of **Blackberries**, *Rubus fruticosus*, often grow 1m (3ft) tall and then arch over and root at the tips, or they may lie prostrate on the ground. This is a prickly plant with a variety of hooked prickles, bristles and glands on stems and leaf stalks. In summer and autumn the white or pink flowers are followed by the familiar blackberries — sweet, juicy, glossy black fruits. Blackberry bushes are found on heaths, in hedgerows and woods throughout the British Isles and Europe.

Raspberry
Rubus idaeus

Raspberry, *Rubus idaeus*, is found throughout the British Isles and most of Europe in woods and on hills, heaths, moors and commons, and in waste places. Its first-year shoots grow up to 2m (6ft) tall and are densely armed with slender prickles and stiff bristles. Around midsummer the second-year shoots produce clusters of white flowers and then the edible raspberries.

Cloudberry, *Rubus chamaemorus*, is a creeping species found in *Sphagnum* bogs and on wet mountain moors in northern Europe and northern Britain. It has erect stems with long-stalked, shallowly lobed leaves and no prickles. Its white flowers appear in summer followed by edible orange fruits.

Cloudberry
Rubus chamaemorus

Pea family

Leguminosae One of the largest families of flowering plants, with about 600 genera and 12,000 species of herbs, shrubs, trees and climbers. Important crop plants include soybeans, lentils, peanuts, peas and beans. Timber comes from trees like acacias. Garden plants include laburnums, brooms, wisterias, sweet peas and lupins.

There are three subfamilies in the Leguminosae, by far the largest in temperate regions being the **Pea subfamily**, the Papilionoideae. The features of this group are: flowers typically pea-like; sepals usually 5, fused into a tube; petals 5, unequal — 1 standard petal at the back, 2 wing petals, and 2 lower petals often joined to form a keel enclosing stamens and ovary; stamens 10, usually 9 fused together and 1 free; ovary superior. Fruit a legume, a pod which splits open along one or both seams. Leaves simple or compound, the latter often with tendrils. Stipules large and leaf-like, small, or modified to form spines. Nodules on the roots contain bacteria which fix nitrogen and supply the plants with nitrates.

Broom, *Cytisus scoparius*, is a shrub growing up to 2m (6ft) tall, with flexible, green, five-angled stems and small, three-leaflet leaves. It bears many yellow flowers in summer followed by black pods which open explosively in hot weather. This plant grows on acid, sandy soils in heaths and woods, waste places and roadsides throughout the British Isles and much of Europe.

Dyer's Greenweed, *Genista tinctoria*, is a much-branched plant 1–2m (3–6ft) tall, with sprawling, smooth green stems

Broom
Cytisus scoparius

Dyer's Greenweed
Genista tinctoria

and stalkless, lance-shaped or pointed-oblong leaves. In late summer yellow flowers appear in the upper leaf axils followed by smooth, flattened pods opening explosively. This plant gets its name from the yellow dye extracted from it, at one time used for dying wool. It grows in pastures and meadows throughout much of Europe, in England, Wales and southern Scotland.

Gorse, *Ulex europaeus*, is a tangled shrub up to 2m (6ft) tall, with branched spines replacing the leaves on older stems. It grows in heaths and grassy places, usually on acid soils, throughout western Europe and the British Isles, flowering from December to June. The smaller Western Gorse, *U. galli*, grows in acid soils, often on heaths, also in western Europe and the British Isles, most commonly in the west. It flowers from July to September, with golden-yellow flowers often tinged with red. Both species produce hairy pods, those of Gorse bursting in summer and those of Western Gorse in spring.

Gorse
Ulex europaeus

The **Milk-vetches** are an extremely large group of about 2000 species in the genus *Astragalus*, found almost worldwide, with over 130 in Europe. These are herbaceous plants with pinnate leaves, racemes of pea-like flowers and oblong or ovoid, often two-celled pods. **Wild Liquorice**, *A. glycyphyllos*, is a straggling perennial with branched stems 30–100cm (1–3ft) tall and many leaves, each with 4–6 pairs of rounded leaflets. In summer the creamy-white or greenish-cream flowers are followed by narrow, slightly curved pods. Plants grow in rough grassy places and scrub across much of Europe and locally throughout Great Britain to central Scotland.

Wild Liquorice
Astragalus glycyphyllos

Pea family

There are over 50 species in the genus *Lathyrus* in Europe, some with winged stems like **Yellow Vetchling**, *L. aphaca*. This is a scrambling annual plant with thin, winged stems up to 1m (3ft) tall. Its leaves have been replaced by coiled tendrils which grow from the axils of large, broadly arrow-shaped stipules. Its flowers are yellow, borne singly on erect stalks in the axils of the stipules. The plant grows in dry, grassy places, often in sandy soils or chalk, across much of Europe, except the north. It has become naturalized in southern England but is not common.

Meadow Vetchling, *Lathyrus pratensis*, is a scrambling perennial plant with thin, angled stems and pinnate leaves, each with one pair of leaflets and a branched tendril; the leaves grow from the axils of arrow-shaped, leaf-like stipules. The flowers are yellow, borne in erect racemes on long stalks in the leaf axils, and followed by compressed black pods. This plant grows in rough grassy places and meadows, on roadsides, in hedgerows and woodland margins throughout Europe and the British Isles.

In **Bitter Vetch**, *Lathyrus montanus*, the leaves lack tendrils but have fine points at the tips instead. This is a perennial creeping plant with erect, winged stems up to 50cm (20in) tall and leaves with 2–4 pairs of elliptical to linear leaflets. It produces loose racemes of crimson flowers on long stalks, the flowers turning blue or green as they age and followed by red-brown, hairless pods. Plants are found in hills and mountains, rough grassland, woods and hedgerows across much of Europe and

Yellow Vetchling
Lathyrus aphaca

Meadow Vetchling
Lathyrus pratensis

Bitter Vetch
Lathyrus montanus

scattered in the British Isles, more commonly in the west.

There are about 55 *Vicia* species in Europe. Some are crop plants, like *V. faba*, the Broad Bean. **Bush Vetch**, *V. sepium*, is a perennial trailing plant with branched, slender stems up to 1m (3ft) tall and pinnate leaves, each with 5−9 pairs of ovate leaflets and a branched tendril. The stipules are half arrow-shaped and usually untoothed. The flowers appear in summer in clusters of 2−6 in the leaf axils; they are pale bluish-purple and followed by black, beaked pods. Plants grow in grassy places, hedgerows and thickets across Europe and the British Isles.

Bush Vetch
Vicia sepium

Tufted Vetch, *Vicia cracca*, is probably one of the most familiar vetches, growing in meadows and fields, along roadsides and in woods throughout Europe and the British Isles. It is a scrambling plant up to 1m (3ft) tall, with pinnate leaves ending in branched tendrils. In summer it produces showy, one-sided racemes of bright bluish-purple flowers growing in the leaf axils. They are followed by squarish pods which crack open in hot summer sun.

Tufted Vetch
Vicia cracca

Some of the *Vicia* species are weeds, like **Hairy Tare**, *V. hirsuta*, once a troublesome weed of grain fields, contaminating the harvest so that the flour was unpalatable. It grows throughout Europe and the British Isles in fields and grassy places. This little, annual plant is often only 30cm (1ft) tall, with branched, slender stems and very narrow leaflets on its pinnate leaves, scrambling through other plants with branched tendrils. In summer it bears small racemes of purplish or whitish flowers.

Hairy Tare
Vicia hirsuta

Common
Restharrow
Ononis repens

Spiny Restharrow
Ononis spinosa

Ribbed Melilot
Melilotus officinalis

Pea family

The **Restharrows**, *Ononis* species, are small shrubs or herbaceous plants. They have simple or clover-like leaves in which the veins end in teeth at the edges of the leaflets, and conspicuous stipules fused to the leaf stalks. There are nearly 50 species in Europe.

Common Restharrow, *Ononis repens*, has woody, branched, often prostrate stems rooting at the base and turning upwards near the tips to grow about 60cm (2ft) tall. Both the stems and the many clover-like leaves are hairy. The plants flower in summer, producing loose, leafy racemes of pinkish-purple flowers in the leaf axils. This plant grows in rough grassy places, on banks, roadsides and in pastures, on dry, calcareous or basic soils across much of Europe; it is scattered throughout the British Isles, becoming rare in western Scotland and western Ireland.

Spiny Restharrow, *Ononis spinosa*, is a similar, slightly taller plant, but its stems do not root at the base, they have two lines of hairs instead of hairs all over and their side shoots end in stiff spines. The leaves have narrow leaflets and the flowers are pink or reddish-purple. This species grows in rough grassy places, on banks, roadsides and pastures on dry, calcareous soils throughout Europe. It is scattered across England, becoming rare in Wales and the southwest.

Ribbed Melilot, *Melilotus officinalis*, is a biennial plant up to 1.5m (5ft) tall, with slender racemes of yellow flowers in late summer. It has clover-like leaves with elliptical, toothed leaflets and a scent of coumarin (new-mown hay), especially when drying. It grows beside roadsides, in waste places and fields throughout continental Europe and has been introduced to the British Isles, where it is common in England and eastern Ireland, rare in Wales and Scotland. **White Melilot**, *M. alba*, with white flowers, also grows in similar places across Europe and has become naturalized in England.

White Melilot
Melilotus alba

Several small, annual *Medicago* species grow in Europe and the British Isles. **Black Medick**, *M. lupulina*, is a branched, trailing, often prostrate plant, sometimes 30cm (1ft) tall or more. It has small, clover-like leaves, heads of minute yellow flowers on long stalks in the leaf axils and ripe pods like tiny black, coiled, kidney-shaped shells. Plants grow in grassy places throughout Europe and the British Isles. Spotted Medick, *M. arabica*, is a larger annual plant with sprawling stems up to 50cm (20in) tall and larger yellow flowers. Its clover-like leaves have dark blotches in the centre of each leaflet and its pods form spiny, round spirals. It grows in grassy and waste places, espcially in sandy soils, across much of Europe, found mostly in southern and eastern England in Britain.

Black Medick
Medicago lupulina

Alfalfa or Lucerne, *Medicago sativa*, is a hairy perennial with erect or sprawling stems up to 90cm (3ft) tall. It has clover-like leaves and racemes of blue-violet flowers followed by pods twisted into a spiral with a hole through the centre. This plant comes from Asia and is cultivated as a forage plant in many parts of Europe, where it has become naturalized in grassy, waste and cultivated places. In the British Isles it is most common in England, more local in Scotland, Wales and Ireland.

Alfalfa
Medicago sativa

Pea family

Bird's-foot Fenugreek, *Trifolium ornithopodioides*, is a branched annual plant 20cm (8in) tall at most, with slender stems and clover-like leaves, each with three oval, serrated leaflets narrowed fowards the base. In summer it produces small clusters of 2–4 pinkish-white flowers on long stalks in the leaf axils, followed by curved pods. This plant grows in dry, sandy and gravelly places, often near the coast in short grassland, in scattered localities around western and southern Europe, England, Wales and eastern Ireland.

Bird's-foot Fenugreek
Trifolium ornithopodioides

Clovers are more familiar members of the genus *Trifolium*. There are nearly 300 species in this genus, mostly found in north temperate regions, with about 100 in Europe. Several are grown as fodder or forage crops. Clovers are, in general, distinguishable from other leguminous plants by their leaves with three leaflets, their stipules joined to the leaf stalks and by their heads or dense, head-like spikes of flowers. The petals, and often the sepals, persist on the flower heads when the pods are formed, becoming brown and withered.

White Clover, *Trifolium repens*, frequently grows in lawns; often unwanted, it is actually useful since the presence of its root nodules improves the soil; it is also grown as a forage plant. In the wild it grows in grassy places, usually on heavy soils, throughout Europe and the British Isles. This is a creeping species with stems which root at the nodes and leaves with three rounded leaflets; there is a white, angled band on each leaflet. The globular heads of white or pinkish flowers grow on long stalks from the

White Clover
Trifolium repens

leaf axils in summer; each head has many flowers and, as in many clovers, the petals are more or less united into a tube with the standard folded around the wings.

Red Clover
Trifolium pratense

Red Clover, *Trifolium pratense*, is grown as a forage crop but wild plants are common in grassy places throughout Europe and the British Isles. This is a variable perennial, forming a straggling clump up to 60cm (2ft) tall, with thin stems and many leaves. Its leaves have narrow, pointed leaflets, often marked with a whitish crescent. The terminal, pink-purple, ovoid heads of flowers are borne between two leaves in summer.

Hare's-foot Clover, *Trifolium arvense*, has striking heads of flowers, silky-hairy from their downy calyces which are longer than the petals. The pink or white flowers are tiny. This is an annual or biennial species, often only 10–20cm (4–8in) tall, with branched stems and leaves with narrow leaflets. It grows in dry, sandy fields and grassy heaths, waste places and roadsides, often on acid soils, sometimes on sand-dunes, throughout Europe and scattered across the British Isles.

Hare's-foot Clover
Trifolium arvense

Hop-trefoil, *Trifolium campestre*, is one of several small *Trifolium* species. These trefoils are straggling, annual or biennial plants with clover-like leaves and tiny heads of yellow flowers in summer, followed by one-seeded pods folded in dried petals. The whole head is supposed to resemble a hop flower, hence the name hop-trefoil. Plants grow 20–30cm (8–12in) tall at most. They are found in dry, grassy places, on roadsides and banks, commons and waste places throughout Europe and the British Isles, rarely in the far north.

Hop-trefoil
Trifolium campestre

Pea family

Bird's-foot Trefoil or Eggs-and-bacon, *Lotus corniculatus*, is found throughout Europe and the British Isles in grassy places, pastures and heaths. It is a small, perennial plant with a clump of slender, leafy stems, which only grow erect if supported by surrounding vegetation, and many compound leaves, each with three leaflets. In summer the plant bears heads of yellow, often red-tinged flowers growing on long stalks from the leaf axils.

Bird's-foot, *Ornithopus perpusillus*, is a prostrate annual plant with slender stems and pinnate leaves. Each leaf has 7–13 pairs of elliptical leaflets, the lowest pair at the base of the leaf stalk and looking like stipules; the real stipules are minute. The flowers are white with red veins; they appear in summer in small clusters subtended by pinnate bracts at the ends of long stalks in the leaf axils. The clusters of pods which follow look like birds' feet; each pod is beaked and segmented and splits into segments rather than splitting open. This little plant grows in dry, sandy and gravelly places, in short grassland and pastures, waste and cultivated ground. It is scattered across much of Europe north to southern Sweden, also across England and Wales, but rare in Scotland and Ireland.

Kidney Vetch or Ladies' Fingers, *Anthyllis vulneraria*, is an old herbal plant used to treat wounds and slow-healing cuts. It is a perennial with sprawling, leafy stems up to 60cm (2ft) tall and pinnate leaves, each leaf with 5–15 pointed-elliptical leaflets, the terminal leaflet much the largest. The flowers are normally yellow, sometimes

Bird's-foot Trefoil
Lotus corniculatus

Bird's-foot
Ornithopus perpusillus

Kidney Vetch
Anthyllis vulneraria

red, turning brown as they fade; their attraction comes not only from their bright colours but also from their white-woolly calyces. They are borne in heads cupped by leaf-like bracts at the ends of erect stems in summer. Plants grow in dry grassland, often on calcareous soils or near the sea, in mountains and on screes, scattered throughout Europe and the British Isles.

Crown Vetch, *Coronilla varia*, is another medicinal plant containing a glycoside that stimulates heart action; because of this it is quite poisonous. It is a straggling, hairless perennial growing up to 1m (3ft) tall, with spreading stems and pinnate leaves. These have 7–12 pairs of elliptical leaflets. The flowers are multicoloured, with a pink standard, whitish wings and a pink, purple-tipped keel; they are borne in heads on long stalks growing from leaf axils in summer. The pods are narrow and four-angled, and they break into segments. This plant grows in grassy places and waste ground across much of Europe; it is naturalized in a number of places in Britain.

Crown Vetch
Coronilla varia

Horseshoe Vetch, *Hippocrepis comosa*, is a variable perennial plant, woody at the base with spreading, branched stems, often prostrate and bearing pinnate leaves on long stalks. The leaves have 7–17 linear to ovate leaflets; in their axils are long stalks with loose, umbel-like clusters of yellow flowers followed by distinctive pods. These are compressed from side to side and twisted into many horseshoe-shaped sections. The plant grows in dry grassland on chalk and limestone, and on sea cliffs across much of Europe, except the north, also in England and rarely in Wales.

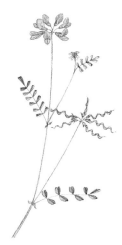

Horseshoe Vetch
Hippocrepis comosa

Flax family

Perennial Flax
Linum perenne

Linaceae About 12 genera and nearly 300 species in this family of herbs and shrubs, found in tropical and temperate regions of the world. Linen and linseed oil come from Cultivated Flax.

Family features Flowers usually borne in cymes or racemes; hermaphrodite, regular. Sepals 5, overlapping; petals 5, contorted, often fleeting; stamens 5, often joined into a ring at the base of the filaments, sometimes alternating with 5 sterile stamens; ovary superior, with 2–6 carpels. Fruits are usually capsules. Leaves simple, usually alternate, with or without stipules.

There are several garden plants in the family, including **Perennial Flax**, *Linum perenne*, with flowers of sky blue. This smooth, blue-green perennial plant has erect, rigid stems 30–90cm (1–3ft) tall and many linear leaves. It bears loose, leafy clusters of flowers around midsummer. In the wild it grows very locally in calcareous grassland in eastern England and in mountain meadows in central and western Europe.

Fairy Flax
Linum catharticum

Fairy Flax, *Linum catharticum*, is a tiny annual plant only 5–20cm (2–8in) tall, with several wiry stems, a few lance-shaped, opposite leaves and numerous, minute white flowers in summer. It grows in grassland, often on calcareous soils, but also on heaths and moors, dunes and cliffs throughout Europe and the British Isles.

Allseed
Radiola linoides

Allseed, *Radiola linoides*, is an even smaller annual, only 8cm (3in) tall at most. Usually its thread-like stems are repeatedly branched, so that it looks more like a chickweed than a flax; it has many elliptical leaves and a multitude of white flowers. It grows on damp, bare patches in sandy or peaty soils on heaths and grassland, locally throughout the British Isles and across much of Europe, except the north.

Wood Sorrel family

Oxalidaceae There are 3 genera and nearly 900 species in this family, mostly herbs, growing in tropical and temperate regions.

   Family features Flowers solitary or in cymes; hermaphrodite, regular. Sepals and petals 5; stamens 10; ovary superior with 5 carpels. Fruits are usually capsules. Leaves compound and clover-like, with 3 rounded leaflets jointed to the leaf stalk; they often exhibit sleep movements by folding downwards at night.

About 800 of the species in this family belong to the genus *Oxalis*. **Wood Sorrel**, *O. acetosella*, forms carpets on shady banks, in woods and hedgerows throughout Europe and the British Isles. Its leaves grow on long stalks 15cm (6in) tall at most; each has three leaflets which fold down at night. The solitary white, lilac-veined flowers appear in spring but produce few seeds. The seeds come mostly from summer flowers which do not open, forming capsules without pollination.

Wood Sorrel
Oxalis acetosella

Procumbent Yellow Sorrel, *Oxalis corniculata*, is a sprawling, annual weed found in gardens and waste places in Europe, most often in England in the British Isles, often present as a variety with purple foliage. It has clover-like leaves which fold down at night and yellow flowers borne in small umbels in the leaf axils.

Procumbent Yellow Sorrel
Oxalis corniculata

Meadow Crane's-bill
Geranium pratense

Bloody Crane's-bill
Geranium sanguineum

Geranium family

Geraniaceae There are 5 genera and about 750 species, mostly herbs, in this small but familiar family. Geraniums are grown in gardens and greenhouses.

Family features Flowers more or less regular and hermaphrodite, with parts in fives. Sepals and petals 5, free, overlapping; stamens 10–15, often joined at the base; ovary superior with 3–5 carpels. Fruits are lobed capsules with 1 seed in each lobe and with stigmas elongated into long beaks. Leaves alternate, simple or compound, often palmately lobed. Stipules present.

Wild Crane's-bills belong to the genus *Geranium*, a group of 300 mainly temperate region species with about 40 in Europe. **Meadow Crane's-bill**, *G. pratense*, grows in meadows and on roadsides throughout much of Europe and Great Britain. It is a perennial plant with clumps of long-stalked, palmately lobed basal leaves and large, blue-violet flowers in summer. The flowers are borne on flowering stalks in loose terminal clusters growing from the axil of a pair of leaves about halfway up each stalk. Within each cluster the flowers grow in pairs. This arrangement of leaves and flowers is characteristic of many crane's-bills. They also have distinctive fruits formed of five spoon-shaped sections with a seed in the bowl of each 'spoon' and all the 'handles' of the spoons forming a 'beak'.

Bloody Crane's-bill, *Geranium sanguineum*, forms clumps of sprawling, leafy stems only 40cm (15in) tall at most. The leaves are rounded or polygonal in outline, deeply lobed, each lobe narrow and cut into three segments. The large, reddish-purple flowers are borne singly. This plant grows among rocks and on fixed dunes, in woods and grassland scattered across much of Europe, in Scotland, northern England, north Wales and western Ireland. It is also grown in gardens.

Several annual crane's-bills are weeds, like **Cut-leaved Crane's-bill**, *Geranium dissectum*. It has branched, straggling stems 60cm (2ft) tall at most, deeply divided leaves and many small, reddish-pink flowers in summer. It is found throughout the British Isles and much of Europe, in cultivated and waste ground, grassland and roadsides.

Cut-leaved Crane's-bill
Geranium dissectum

Herb Robert, *Geranium robertianum*, has palmate, almost ferny leaves with a disagreeable scent, turning red in the sun or in autumn. This is an annual, often hairy plant with branched, straggling stems growing about 30cm (1ft) tall and small pink flowers. Plants grow in hedges and woods, among rocks or on crumbling walls, on shingle near the coast throughout Europe and the British Isles.

Herb Robert
Geranium robertianum

Stork's-bills, members of the genus *Erodium*, come mostly from the Mediterranean, but **Common Stork's-bill**, *E. cicutarium*, grows throughout Europe and much of Great Britain, near the sea in Ireland. It is found in dry grassland, waste places and arable land, usually in sandy soils, often in dunes. This annual plant has rosettes of ferny, pinnate leaves at first, then prostrate, branched, leafy stems with umbels of pink flowers. The fruits are similar to those of crane's-bills, but with much longer 'handles' to the 'spoons'. They split into single-seeded sections, the beaks remaining attached to the seeds and becoming coiled like corkscrews.

Common
Stork's-bill
Erodium cicutarium

Touch-me-not family

Balsaminaceae This family has 4 genera and 600 species, over 500 in the genus *Impatiens*. They are mostly found in tropical Asia and Africa. Busy-Lizzies are popular house and garden plants.

Family features Flowers often drooping, solitary or borne in racemes; hermaphrodite, bilaterally symmetrical. Sepals 3–5, often petal-like, one larger than the others and spurred; petals 5, the largest uppermost, the 2 on each side usually fused together; stamens 5, alternating with the petals; ovary superior with 5 cells. Fruit a capsule; when ripe a light touch will trigger fruits into opening. Leaves simple.

Policeman's Helmet
Impatiens glandulifera

Policeman's Helmet, *Impatiens glandulifera*, has been brought to Europe from the Himalayas and is now colonizing riverbanks in many areas, including the British Isles. It is a hairless annual plant with stout, translucent stems 1–2m (3–6ft) tall, its elliptical or lance-shaped, serrated leaves borne in opposite pairs or in whorls. The large flowers are like pinkish-purple helmets, borne in clusters on drooping stalks in the upper leaf axils. They are followed by pear-shaped fruits that explode on touch when ripe.

Small Balsam
Impatiens parviflora

Small Balsam, *Impatiens parviflora*, is another Asian plant naturalized in shady waste places and woods across much of Europe, including England and Wales. It is an annual, 30–90cm (1–3ft) tall, with alternate, pointed-ovate, serrated leaves. The flowers are small and pale yellow, borne in clusters in the leaf axils and followed by explosive, club-shaped capsules. The similar **Touch-me-not**,

Touch-me-not
Impatiens noli-tangere

I. noli-tangere, is a native plant, with broader leaves and larger, bright yellow flowers spotted with brown. It grows beside streams and ditches, in wet woods and ravines across much of Europe, in the Lake District in Britain.

Milkwort family

Polygalaceae About 12 genera and 800 species of herbs, shrubs and climbers found in temperate and tropical regions throughout many parts of the world.

Family features Flowers often borne on jointed stalks, hermaphrodite, bilaterally symmetrical. Sepals 5, free, inner 2 often petal-like and resembling wings; petals 3−5, outer 2 free or united with the lowermost, 2 upper free or absent; stamens usually 8, their filaments often joined into a sheath which is split above and joined to the petals; ovary superior, usually with 2 cells. Fruit a capsule or fleshy. Leaves simple, usually alternate. Stipules 0.

Common Milkwort
Polygala vulgaris

About 30 **Milkworts**, *Polygala* species, are found in Europe. **Common Milkwort**, *P. vulgaris*, is a small perennial up to 30cm (1ft) tall, with branched stems and alternate, narrowly ovate leaves. The flowers are borne in terminal racemes in early summer. They may be blue, pink or white, with greenish outer sepals and inner sepals the same colour as the petals. Plants grow in chalk and limestone grassland, on heaths and dunes throughout Europe and the British Isles. **Heath Milkwort**, *P. serpyllifolia*, is a more delicate, slender plant in which at least the lower leaves are opposite. It usually has blue flowers. It grows in acid soils, on heaths and in other grassy places in western and central Europe and throughout the British Isles.

Heath Milkwort
Polygala serpyllifolia

Spurge family

Euphorbiaceae A very large family of trees, shrubs and herbs, mostly tropical, with about 300 genera and 5000 species. Economically important products include rubber, castor oil and tapioca.

Family features Flowers regular, unisexual, males and females often on the same plant. Sepals usually present, petals usually absent, but both may be missing; stamens one to many; ovary superior with 3 cells. Fruit a capsule or drupe. Leaves usually simple, alternate. Stipules usually present.

Dog's Mercury
Mercurialis perennis

Dog's Mercury, *Mercurialis perennis*, is a poisonous perennial plant found throughout Europe and much of Great Britain. Its erect, leafy stems carpet the floor of deciduous woods in spring, especially beech woods on chalk, or grow in shady hedgerows and among mountain rocks. Each stem grows 15–40cm (6–15in) tall and has opposite, lance-shaped leaves crowded near the top. Green male and female flowers grow on separate plants, females singly or in small clusters on long stalks, males in erect, tassel-like spikes.

Sun Spurge
Euphorbia helioscopia

The **Spurges**, *Euphorbia* species, are a vast group of 2000 herbs, shrubs and trees, spread throughout the tropics and warmer temperate regions of the world, with over 100 in Europe. Their flowers are very reduced, the males consisting of a single stamen, the females of a single pistil. Several male flowers are arranged around one female and together they form the centre of a cup-like bract, the whole arrangement looking like one flower. These are grouped into clusters with special leaves beneath. Spurges have white, milky sap, often caustic and sometimes poisonous.

Some spurges are weeds, like the **Sun Spurge**, *Euphorbia helioscopia*, found in cultivated ground, gardens and waste places throughout Europe and the British Isles. It is a hairless annual plant with a single leafy stem 20–50cm (8–20in) tall ending in umbels of flowers cupped in broad, leafy, often bright yellow bracts. Leaves and bracts are all finely toothed on the ends.

Petty Spurge, *Euphorbia peplus*, is another weedy annual found in cultivated ground and waste places throughout the British Isles and Europe. It is a leafy plant, no more than 30cm (1ft) tall, its stem often branched to form loose, leafy umbels of flowers. Like other spurges it was at one time used in herb medicine, a practice largely discontinued because its acrid sap is corrosive and dangerous.

Petty Spurge
Euphorbia peplus

Cypress Spurge, *Euphorbia cyparissias*, is a perennial, hairless plant with creeping rhizomes and many erect, branched stems only 30cm (1ft) tall and dense, linear leaves. Flowers grow at the tops of the stems, the yellow-green leaves of the umbels round and turning red in the sun or with age. This plant grows in cultivated land, beside roads, in scrub, grassy and rocky places in Europe, mostly in gardens or as a casual weed of waste places in Britain.

Cypress Spurge
Euphorbia cyparissias

Wood Spurge, *Euphorbia amygdaloides*, is a clump-forming perennial, its stems sterile with dark green leaves at the top in the first year, flowering in the second. The flowers are borne in umbels, the yellowish bracts beneath each umbel joined into pairs. Plants grow in damp woods across Europe, except in the north, mainly in southern England and Wales in Great Britain.

Wood Spurge
Euphorbia amygdaloides

Mallow family

Malvaceae About 75 genera and 1000 species of herbs, shrubs and trees from tropical and temperate regions. The family includes plants grown for fibres, like cotton, and others for ornament, like hibiscus and hollyhocks.

Family features Flowers solitary or borne in branched racemes; regular, hermaphrodite. Sepals 5, often united (an epicalyx is often present also); petals 5, more or less separate; stamens numerous, joined at the base to form a tube; ovary superior with 2 to many carpels. Fruit a capsule or schizocarpic, i.e. splitting into many one-seeded sections. Leaves alternate, entire or palmately lobed. Stipules present. The plants are often velvety in texture with star-shaped hairs.

Common Mallow
Malva sylvestris

Musk Mallow
Malva moschata

About 13 **Mallows**, *Malva* species, grow in Europe. **Common Mallow**, *M. sylvestris*, is a conspicuous perennial plant of dry roadsides and waste places, grassland and hedgerows, found throughout Europe and much of the British Isles. It has sprawling stems up to 90cm (3ft) tall, with long-stalked, shallowly lobed, heart-shaped or kidney-shaped leaves. In summer its pink-purple, dark-veined flowers appear in the leaf axils. Like other mallows, this plant has fruits like round cheeses cut into segments. The base of the fruit is formed from the receptacle cupped in the calyx, and the segments are formed from a flat ring of nutlets (wrinkled and brownish-green in this species).

Musk Mallow, *Malva moschata*, grows on the edges of fields and meadows, in hedgerows and on roadsides throughout Europe and Great Britain. It is a musk-scented perennial plant with branched, hairy stems up to 90cm (3ft) tall, kidney-shaped basal leaves and divided stem leaves, the topmost with linear segments. The rose-pink or purple flowers are mostly borne in dense, terminal clusters and followed by rounded, densely hairy fruits.

Dwarf Mallow
Malva neglecta

Dwarf Mallow, *Malva neglecta*, is a smaller, annual mallow with prostrate or sprawling, branched stems up to 60cm (2ft) tall. Its stems are downy and its leaves long-stalked with palmately lobed blades. Flowers appear in the leaf axils in summer; they are whitish, veined or tinged with lilac, with notched petals.

Marsh Mallow, *Althaea officinalis*, is a grey-velvety, perennial plant up to 120cm (4ft) tall, with triangular, toothed leaves, the upper ones folded like fans. The pink flowers appear in the upper leaf axils in late summer. Plants grow in salt marshes and on the sides of ditches near the sea, in Europe north to the southern coasts of the British Isles. The roots of this plant are rich in mucilage and were used to make the original marshmallows. They are still used in herb medicine to soothe intestinal disorders and in poultices.

Marsh Mallow
Althaea officinalis

Tree Mallow, *Lavatera arborea*, is a large biennial plant — in its second, flowering year it reaches 3m (9ft) in height and has many branched stems with large, rounded, shallowly lobed, long-stalked leaves. Its purple, dark-veined flowers are followed by rings of yellowish, wrinkled nutlets. This plant grows in rocky places and waste ground near the sea on the Mediterranean and Atlantic coasts of Europe north to the south and west coasts of the British Isles; it is introduced elsewhere.

Tree Mallow
Lavatera arborea

Sweet Violet
Viola odorata

Common Dog-violet
Viola riviniana

Marsh Violet
Viola palustris

Violet family

Violaceae About 22 genera and 900 species of herbs, mostly from temperate and tropical regions. Violets and pansies are grown in gardens.

Family features Flowers solitary or borne in racemes; hermaphrodite, regular or bilaterally symmetrical. Sepals 5; petals 5, usually unequal and the lowermost spurred; stamens 5, the lower 2 often spurred at the base and with the anthers of all 5 joined around the ovary; ovary superior with 1 cell. Fruit a capsule or berry. Leaves simple, alternate, with leafy stipules.

There are over 90 *Viola* species in Europe out of a total of 500 worldwide. Violets are small plants which produce spurred, bilaterally symmetrical flowers with five petals in spring. In summer they produce flowers which are hidden beneath the foliage, do not open and which are self-pollinated.

Sweet Violets, *Viola odorata*, grow about 20cm (8in) tall, forming rosettes of long-stalked, broadly heart-shaped leaves and long, leafless runners which produce new plants. Their sweet-scented, deep purple or white flowers open in spring and the closed flowers are produced all summer beneath the leaves. Sweet Violets grow in coppiced woods, in hedgerows, thickets and plantations, usually on calcareous soils, throughout Europe, in England, Wales and central Ireland. They are also grown in gardens and used in herbal remedies for coughs and colds and in headache treatments.

Common Dog-violet, *Viola riviniana*, is abundant throughout Europe and the British Isles in open woods, hedgerows, heaths and pastures. It is a perennial plant, often only 15cm (6in) tall with a clump of long-stalked, heart-shaped leaves. The solitary spring flowers are blue-violet with a paler spur.

Marsh Violet, *Viola palustris*, has slender rhizomes with long-stalked leaves growing from the nodes; these have broad, almost kidney-shaped blades. The solitary spring flowers are lilac with darker veins. This little plant grows in marshes, wet heaths and bogs, in acid soils across much of Europe and the British Isles.

Yellow Wood Violet
Viola biflora

Yellow Wood Violet, *Viola biflora*, grows in damp, shady woods or among rocks in the mountains of western Europe but not in the British Isles. It is a delicate plant with slender, leafy stems bearing kidney-shaped leaves on long stalks and pairs of golden-yellow flowers veined with brown.

Pansies do not have closed flowers but instead go on producing showy flowers all summer. **Wild Pansy** or Heartsease, *Viola tricolor*, has much smaller flowers but the same sprawling, leafy stems as Garden Pansies. It has two subspecies: *tricolor* is an annual with blue-violet flowers, found in cultivated and waste ground across most of Europe and the British Isles; *curtisii* is a perennial with blue-violet, yellow or multicoloured flowers, found on dunes and in grassy places on British and European coasts.

Wild Pansy
Viola tricolor

Field Pansy, *Viola arvensis*, has sprawling, branched, leafy stems like a Wild Pansy, but small, creamy-white flowers, often with blue-tinged upper petals. It grows in waste places and cultivated land throughout Europe and the British Isles.

Field Pansy
Viola arvensis

St John's-wort family

Hypericaceae About 8 genera and 400 species of herbs, shrubs and trees in this family, many from temperate regions of the world. Some are grown in gardens.

Common St John's-wort
Hypericum perforatum

Many herbaceous and shrubby **St John's-worts**, *Hypericum* species, grow in Europe, recognizable from their showy yellow flowers with five sepals and petals and numerous stamens. **Common St John's-wort**, *H. perforatum*, is a perennial, herbaceous species found in hedgebanks, open woods and rough grassland throughout Europe and much of the British Isles. It has branched stems about 60cm (2ft) tall and opposite, linear leaves covered by translucent dots. The flowers are borne in a large inflorescence on stems growing from the upper leaf axils. The petals have black dots on their edges.

Rockrose family

Cistaceae About 8 genera and 200 species of herbs and shrubs, many found in the Mediterranean region. Some are grown in gardens.

Common Rockrose
Helianthemum nummularium

    Family features Flowers regular, hermaphrodite. Sepals 3 or 5, free; petals 5, free, often contorted, soon falling; stamens numerous, free; ovary superior. Fruit a capsule. Leaves usually opposite, simple.

Mare's-tail
Hippuris vulgaris

Common Rockrose, *Helianthemum nummularium*, has sprawling stems up to 30cm (1ft) tall, with oblong leaves and yellow flowers in summer. Plants grow in dry, basic grassland, often among rocks or on banks, throughout Europe and most of Great Britain.

Mare's-tail family

Hippuridaceae The only species in this family is **Mare's-tail**, *Hippuris vulgaris*, found in lakes, ponds and quiet streams throughout the British Isles and Europe. This is a perennial plant, with erect stems projecting well above the water surface. The stems are leafy, with whorls of 6–12 linear leaves above and beneath the water. In summer plants bear tiny flowers in the upper leaf axils; they have no sepals or petals and either have a single stamen with a one-celled ovary beneath, or one stamen alone. The fruits are smooth green achenes.

Water-milfoil family

Haloragidaceae About 7 genera and 170 species, mostly aquatic and marsh plants, found throughout the world.

Spiked Water-milfoil
Myriophyllum spicatum

There are five species of **Water-milfoils** in Europe, belonging to the genus *Myriophyllum*. They are aquatic herbs with erect stems and whorls of dissected leaves. The small flowers are borne in terminal spikes, often with male flowers at the top, females below. **Spiked Water-milfoil**, *M. spicatum*, grows in lakes, ditches and streams scattered throughout the British Isles and much of Europe. It has branched stems with whorls of 3–4 leaves beneath the water and emergent, almost leafless flowering stems with whorls of tiny, reddish flowers. **Whorled Water-milfoil**, *M. verticillatum,* grows in lakes and ponds in lowland areas of Europe and Great Britain. Its leaves are borne in whorls of five, those below the water larger than those on the flowering spikes which emerge above the surface.

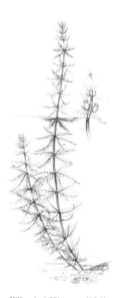

Whorled Water-milfoil
Myriophyllum verticillatum

Willowherb family

Onagraceae About 20 genera and 650 species of herbs and shrubs, found most commonly in the temperate regions.

Family features Flowers hermaphrodite, bilaterally symmetrical or more or less regular. Sepals 2, 4 or 5, free but with calyx-tube attached to the ovary; petals 2, 4 or 5, free; stamens as many as or twice as many as sepals; ovary usually inferior, with 2–5 cells. Fruit usually a capsule or berry but may be indehiscent. Leaves simple, opposite, alternate or whorled. Stipules often 0.

Rosebay Willowherb
Chamaenerion angustifolium

Great Hairy Willowherb
Epilobium hirsutum

Rosebay Willowherb, *Chamaenerion angustifolium*, is one of the most easily recognized willowherbs, with colonies of erect, leafy stems growing up to 2m (6ft) tall and topped by spikes of red-purple flowers in mid and late summer. The flowers are followed by long capsules which split open to reveal silky-haired seeds. Until 50 years ago this was a local mountain plant but since then it has spread across Europe and the British Isles, becoming common in waste places and open woods, on roadsides and riverbanks, in cities and open countryside.

Most **Willowherbs** belong to the genus *Epilobium*, a large group with over 100 species (about 25 in Europe), found throughout the world, except in the tropics. The European species are perennials with pink or purple flowers, many found in wet places, beside rivers, in marshes and damp woods, others as weeds in disturbed habitats.

Great Hairy Willowherb, *Epilobium hirsutum*, grows beside ponds and rivers, in marshes and fens throughout Europe and much of Great Britain. It forms erect, leafy stems up to 1.5m (5ft) tall, with lance-shaped, softly hairy, toothed leaves and attractive flowers at the tops of elongated ovaries in summer.

Evening Primrose, *Oenothera biennis*, is native to North America but has become naturalized in waste places in England and parts of Europe. It is a biennial plant, with a rosette of lance-shaped, often wavy leaves in the first year and a leafy flowering stem up to 1.5m (5ft) tall in the second. The scented, showy yellow flowers open in the evening and are followed by large, oblong capsules. This is the plant from which comes Evening Primrose oil.

Evening Primrose
Oenothera biennis

Hedge Fuchsia, *Fuchsia magellanica*, was introduced to the British Isles as a hedge plant, growing most vigorously in the west and in Ireland, escaping into the wild in some places. It is a shrub, reaching 3m (9ft) tall or so in warmer situations, but cut to the ground each winter and only 90cm (3ft) tall in colder areas. It has arching stems, toothed, oval leaves and many pendent flowers in the leaf axils in summer. The flowers have reddish stems, red calyx-tubes and red sepals, purple petals and long, protruding stamens and style.

Hedge Fuchsia
Fuchsia magellanica

Enchanter's Nightshade, *Circaea lutetiana*, forms colonies in woods, hedgerows and shady places across most of Europe and the British Isles. It has erect stems up to 60cm (2ft) tall, with pointed-ovate leaves near the base and sparse, elongated racemes of tiny white flowers in late summer. The flowers point downwards on long stalks; each has two sepals, two petals and two stamens. The fruits are bristly capsules pointing downwards on long stalks like the flowers before them.

Enchanter's Nightshade
Circaea lutetiana

Loosestrife family

Lythraceae About 25 genera and 550 species of herbs and shrubs found almost worldwide. Henna comes from a member of this family.

Family features Flowers solitary or borne in complex clusters; hermaphrodite and regular. Calyx tubular, usually with five teeth; petals 4–6, free, often crumpled in bud; stamens 2–12, often as many as or twice as many as the petals; ovary superior with 2–4 cells. Fruits usually capsules. Leaves usually whorled or opposite. Stipules minute or 0.

Purple Loosestrife
Lythrum salicaria

Purple Loosestrife, *Lythrum salicaria*, is found across most of the northern hemisphere in marshes, beside streams and lakes. This perennial plant has tall, unbranched flowering stems, conspicuous in late summer with their reddish-purple flowers. The flower spikes are formed of many whorls of flowers, each with six crumpled petals.

Cucumber family

Cucurbitaceae About 100 genera and 900 species, mostly tropical herbs and vines. There are many economically important species in this family, like melons, marrows and cucumbers.

Few species are found in Europe.
White Bryony or Red Bryony, *Bryonia cretica*, is a bristly climber, with long, angled, branched stems, palmately lobed leaves and coiled tendrils. Male and female flowers grow in the leaf axils on separate plants; they have spreading sepals and five greenish-white, net-veined petals, but male flowers have three stamens, females have three stigmas and an inferior ovary. The

White Bryony
Bryonia cretica

fruits are red berries. This plant
scrambles about in hedgerows, scrub
and woodland margins, usually on
calcareous soils, across much of Europe,
in England and eastern Wales.

Ivy family

Araliaceae A mostly tropical family of
55 genera and about 700 species, chiefly
trees and shrubs. One of the most
famous family members is Ginseng.

Ivy, *Hedera helix*, is the only member of
the family found wild in Europe. It is
an evergreen, woody climber, growing
in woods and shady places, climbing on
trees, rocks and walls or creeping over
the ground. Its leaves are dark green
and glossy, shade leaves with 3–5 lobes,
those in sun elliptical and lacking lobes
or teeth. Umbels of flowers are borne
by sunlit plants; each bloom has a five-
toothed calyx, a five-lobed, yellow-green
corolla, five stamens and an inferior
ovary. They are followed by black
berries. Ivy is poisonous.

Ivy
Hedera helix

Dogwood family

Cornaceae A small family, mainly of
trees and shrubs, with 12 genera and
about 100 species, most from northern
temperate regions.

Dwarf Cornel, *Cornus suecica*, is a
creeping plant with erect stems up to
20cm (8in) tall and opposite pairs of
stalkless, ovate leaves. At the top of
each stem is an umbel of tiny, dark
purple flowers subtended by four large,
oval, white bracts. The fruits are red,
egg-shaped drupes. This plant grows on
moors, heaths and mountains in
northern Europe, locally in the Scottish
Highlands, rarely in northern England.

Dwarf Cornel
Cornus suecica

Carrot family

Umbelliferae Also known as the
Parsley family and the Apiaceae. A large
family of herbaceous plants, with about
275 genera and 2850 species, mostly
from northern temperate regions. Many
kitchen herbs, like parsley, fennel,
caraway and coriander, come from this
family, together with vegetables like
celery and carrots. Some species,
including Hemlock, are very poisonous.

Family features Flowers tiny,
regular and hermaphrodite, usually
borne in simple or compound umbels,
sometimes in heads. Calyx 5-lobed,
fused to the ovary; petals 5, free, soon
falling; stamens 5, alternating with
petals; ovary inferior with 2 cells. Fruit
consists of 2 sections, one each side of a
central axis, often joined together and
suspended across the top of this axis.
Leaves alternate, usually compound and
often divided, with sheathing bases.
Stipules 0. Many species are aromatic.

Marsh Pennywort
Hydrocotyle vulgaris

Sanicle
Sanicula europaea

Marsh Pennywort, *Hydrocotyle
vulgaris*, grows in marshes, fens and
bogs, beside streams and in wet
meadows, often on acid soils,
throughout the British Isles and much
of Europe. It is a perennial plant with
slender, creeping stems and long-
stalked, shallowly lobed, round leaves
with a dimple in the centre where the
stalk joins at the back. The tiny,
pinkish-green flowers are borne in
whorl-like umbels on separate stalks.

Sanicle, *Sanicula europaea*, forms large
colonies in deciduous woodland, often
on calcareous soils, throughout the
British Isles and Europe. This perennial
plant has a clump of shiny, palmately
lobed leaves, and flowering stems up to
60cm (2ft) tall in summer. The latter

bear small, dense umbels of pink or white flowers, hermaphrodite in the centre, male on the outside. The fruits are covered with hooked bristles.

Sea-holly, *Eryngium maritimum*, is an unusual umbellifer. It is a blue-grey perennial plant with leathery, spiny-lobed, white-veined basal leaves and flowering stems up to 60cm (2ft) tall in late summer, also with spiny leaves. The metallic blue flowers are borne in terminal clusters of heads cupped in spiny bracts. Plants grow on sandy beaches, dunes and shingle banks on the coasts of the British Isles and western Europe, north to southern Scandinavia.

Sea-holly
Eryngium maritimum

Rough Chervil, *Chaerophyllum temulentum*, is a hairy biennial plant, with a clump of twice- or three-times pinnate leaves in the first year, and leafy flowering stems up to 1m (3ft) tall in the second. The stems are solid and purple-spotted and the leaves turn purple as they age; the umbels of white flowers are nodding in bud, each with several narrow bracts beneath and 8−10 rays. This is a poisonous plant found in hedgerows across most of Europe and much of the British Isles, coming into bloom just after Cow Parsley.

Rough Chervil
Chaerophyllum temulentum

Cow Parsley, *Anthriscus sylvestris*, blooms in early summer in hedges, woodland margins and waste places throughout most of the British Isles and Europe. It is another biennial plant, with twice- to three-times pinnate leaves in the first year, and leafy, furrowed flowering stems up to 1m (3ft) tall in the second, with many compound umbels of white flowers. Each umbel has 6−12 rays, 4−6 narrow bracts and an outer ring of flowers with enlarged outside petals.

Cow Parsley
Anthriscus sylvestris

Carrot family

Venus' Comb
Scandix pecten-veneris

Venus' Comb, *Scandix pecten-veneris*, is a once common but now rare weed of arable land, found across Europe and in southeastern England. It is an annual plant with an erect, branched stem up to 60cm (2ft tall), and twice- to three-times pinnate, ferny leaves. The small white flowers are borne in simple umbels, usually growing in pairs in early summer. The plant becomes highly distinctive when the fruits form, for they are 1.5 – 8cm (½ – 3in) long with extremely long beaks.

Sweet Cicely, *Myrrhis odorata*, is a perennial plant with hollow, grooved stems up to 2m (6ft) tall and twice- or three-times pinnate leaves with serrated segments. It flowers in early summer, with compound umbels of white flowers, some with hermaphrodite flowers, others with male flowers only and these with shorter, more slender rays. The outer flowers of each umbel have unequal petals. The ripe fruits are shiny brown and ridged with bristly hairs. Plants grow in grassy places, hedges and woods, in hills and mountains across Europe and in northern areas of the British Isles. The leaves and fruits are edible and taste of aniseed.

Sweet Cicely
Myrrhis odorata

Alexanders
Smyrnium olusatrum

Alexanders, *Smyrnium olusatrum*, grows on cliffs, in waste places, woods and hedgebanks, mainly near the sea but also inland. It comes originally from the Mediterranean region, but has become naturalized northwards to Holland and the British Isles. At one time it was eaten as a vegetable. This is a stout biennial plant, its furrowed, second-year stems growing up to 1.5m (5ft) tall and branching to produce dense, rounded umbels of yellow-green flowers in early summer. Each compound umbel has 7–15 rays. The leaves are shiny, basal ones up to 30cm (1ft) long and three-times divided into three leaflets; all the leaves have broadly sheathing bases.

Pignut
Conopodium majus

Pignut or Earthnut, *Conopodium majus*, is a slender perennial plant found in woods and fields on acid soils in much of western Europe and the British Isles. It grows from a dark brown, irregular tuber (edible and with a nutty taste), producing broad, twice-pinnate basal leaves which soon wither, and sending up a slender stem about 50cm (20in) tall, its upper leaves finely divided with linear segments. It flowers in early summer, producing compound umbels with 6–12 rays and white flowers, their petals unequal on the margins.

Burnet Saxifrage, *Pimpinella saxifraga*, is another relatively slender perennial, this one scattered across most of Europe and the British Isles in dry, grassy places, often on calcareous soils. It has an erect stem, rough in texture and solid, with pinnate leaves and serrated leaflets, the lower leaves twice-pinnate. It blooms in late summer; its flat-topped, compound umbels have 10–22 rays and white flowers.

Burnet Saxifrage
Pimpinella saxifraga

Ground Elder, *Aegopodium podagraria*, was used in herb medicine at one time to treat gout and rheumatism. It was also grown in gardens for its leaves which were eaten like spinach, and still grows as a weed in gardens and waste places across much of Europe and the British Isles. It sends up carpets of pinnate leaves in spring, with erect flowering stems in summer. These bear dense, rounded umbels of white flowers, with 10–20 rays in each umbel.

Ground Elder
Aegopodium podagraria

Carrot family

Lesser Water Parsnip
Berula erecta

Lesser Water Parsnip, *Berula erecta*, grows in ditches and canals, marshes and ponds across much of Europe and lowland areas of the British Isles, rarely in Wales and Scotland. It has hollow, sprawling stems which root where they touch the ground or the mud beneath the water, pinnate leaves with serrated leaflets and umbels of white flowers in late summer. The umbels are rather irregular, with 7–18 rays and leaf-like, often three-lobed bracts.

Rock Samphire, *Crithmum maritimum*, is a coastal plant, most often growing on cliffs and rocks around the Atlantic and Mediterranean coasts of Europe, around Ireland and on the western and southern coasts of England. It is a branched, perennial, blue-grey plant, with solid, narrowly ridged stems and fleshy, pinnate leaves with narrow leaflets. Yellow-green flowers appear after midsummer, borne in stout umbels with 8–36 rays. Young leaves, stems and seedpods can all be pickled.

Rock Samphire
Crithmum maritimum

The **Water-dropworts** are a group of about 35 perennial, aquatic or marsh species in the genus *Oenanthe*, with 13 in Europe. Some are poisonous, like **Tubular Water-dropwort**, *O. fistulosa*, found in marshes and shallow water across most of Europe, mainly in the east in the British Isles. It has erect, hollow stems 30–90cm (1–3ft) tall, constricted at the nodes and growing from a clump of swollen, spindle-shaped roots. The leaves are pinnate with tubular leaf stalks and linear leaflets, and the white flowers are borne in late summer in dense umbels with 2–4 rays. The partial umbels become globular in fruit. Hemlock Water-dropwort, *O.*

Tubular Water-dropwort
Oenanthe fistulosa

crocata, is one of the most deadly umbellifers; its stems may be mistaken for celery and its roots for parsnips. It grows in acid soils in wet, grassy places, on woodland edges, in ditches and beside water in western Europe and Ireland. Its erect stems are hollow and grooved, up to 1.5m (5ft) tall, and its leaves are large and ferny with serrated leaflets and sheathing bases. Plants flower around midsummer, bearing large, terminal umbels with 10–40 rays and white flowers.

So many of the poisonous umbellifers resemble the edible ones that it is risky to eat wild plants. **Fool's Parsley**, *Aethusa cynapium*, is a potentially lethal umbellifer which may be mistaken for Parsley, but it has a foetid scent. It grows as a weed of arable land, gardens and waste places throughout most of Europe and the British Isles. This is a hairless annual plant, with branched, leafy stems, twice-pinnate leaves with leaflets in threes and umbels of white flowers in the latter half of summer. Each umbel has 10–20 rays and three or four linear bracts hang beneath one side of each partial umbel.

Fool's Parsley
Aethusa cynapium

Fennel, *Foeniculum vulgare*, is a salad plant and vegetable with an anise-like scent and taste. It is native to the Mediterranean region but also cultivated and naturalized across much of Europe, less commonly in England and Ireland. It grows in waste places and on roadsides, on cliffs near the sea. This is a hairless, perennial plant with an erect, solid stem up to 2m (6ft) tall and extremely finely divided leaves with linear segments. Opposite the upper leaves are long stalks bearing compound umbels of yellow flowers each with 10–40 rays and no bracts.

Fennel
Foeniculum vulgare

Carrot family

Hemlock, *Conium maculatum*, is a potentially lethal plant, famous for its part in the death of Socrates. It grows throughout Europe and the British Isles in damp places and often on heavy soils, in woods and meadows, fields and roadsides, beside ditches and streams. It is a biennial, with a branched, furrowed flowering stem up to 3m (9ft) tall in the second year, distinctive for its smooth texture, greyish colour and purple spots. It has a foetid scent likened to that of mice, and soft, twice- to four-times pinnate leaves with coarsely serrated leaflets. The umbels of white flowers appear around midsummer.

Hemlock
Conium maculatum

Hare's-ear or Thorow-wax, *Bupleurum rotundifolium*, is one of about 40 *Bupleurum* species in Europe, all with simple leaves. It is an annual plant with an erect, hollow, often purple-tinged stem, 30cm (1ft) tall, with round leaves, the upper ones encircling the stem. Yellow flowers are borne in compound umbels with 4–8 rays; each partial umbel is cupped in conspicuous, broad, yellow-green bracts. This little plant grows in arable land and waste places in western and central Europe.

Fool's Watercress, *Apium nodiflorum*, is not poisonous, even though its name implies danger. It is found in western and southern Europe and much of the British Isles, most commonly in the south, growing in shallow ponds and ditches, often with Watercress; the leaves of the two plants are similar and both are edible. This is a sprawling plant, with furrowed stems and shiny, bright green, pinnate leaves with ovate leaflets. The white flowers appear in late summer in small, compound

Hare's-ear
Bupleurum rotundifolium

umbels, each with 3−15 rays; there are 4−7 small bracts beneath each partial umbel. Wild Celery, *A. graveolens*, is like a strong-flavoured, wild version of cultivated celery, found locally in damp places, especially in brackish soil near the sea, in Europe north to Denmark and in maritime counties of the British Isles. It is a biennial plant, with erect, grooved stems, yellow-green pinnate leaves and dense, compound umbels of greenish-white flowers.

Fool's Watercress
Apium nodiflorum

Parsley, *Petroselinum crispum*, is a stout biennial plant with branched, solid stems up to 75cm (30in) tall and shiny, three-times pinnate leaves, often crisped at the edges and with the characteristic parsley scent. The plant produces flat-topped umbels of yellowish flowers around midsummer; the umbels are compound, with 8−20 rays. Parsley grows wild and is cultivated as a kitchen herb throughout Europe and the British Isles, except in northern Scotland, growing on rocks and walls, in waste and grassy places. However, it is not wise to eat wild plants because they may be mistaken for Fool's Parsley.

Parsley
Petroselinum crispum

Cowbane, *Cicuta virosa*, is an extremely poisonous plant found locally in ditches and marshes in Great Britain and parts of northern Ireland, northern and central Europe. Its deadly roots are most likely to be found on the banks of cleaned ditches and may be mistaken for parsnips since they have a similar scent. Cowbane is a stout, perennial plant with hollow stems up to 120cm (4ft) tall, large, twice- or three-times pinnate leaves with linear or lance-shaped segments, and dense umbels of white flowers in late summer. Each umbel has 10−30 rays and many small, linear bracts beneath each partial umbel.

Cowbane
Cicuta virosa

Carrot family

Lovage
*Levisticum
officinale*

Lovage, *Levisticum officinale*, is a culinary and medicinal herb, originally from Iran but now naturalized throughout much of Europe, sometimes in the British Isles. It is an aromatic perennial, with hollow, branched stems up to 2.5m (8ft) tall, large, shiny green leaves, twice- or three-times pinnate with irregularly toothed, wedge-shaped segments, and umbels of yellowish flowers in late summer. The umbels measure up to 20cm (8in) across and have 12–20 rays.

Wild Angelica, *Angelica sylvestris*, has hollow, finely ribbed stems up to 2m (6ft) tall, often purple-tinged and with a whitish bloom. Its lower leaves grow up to 60cm (2ft) long and are twice- or three-times pinnate with serrated segments; upper leaves are reduced to inflated sheaths. The white or pink flowers are borne in large umbels with 15–40 rays. Plants grow in damp meadows, woods and fens throughout Europe and the British Isles.

Wild Angelica
Angelica sylvestris

Wild Parsnip, *Pastinaca sativa*, is the wild form of the cultivated plant and has a strong parsnip scent. It is a biennial, with pinnate, basal leaves in the first year and leafy flowering stems up to 1.5m (5ft) tall in the second. These stems are hollow and furrowed, with dense, compound umbels of tiny yellow flowers in late summer. Each flower has five inrolled petals. Plants grow in grassy waste places and along roadsides, often on chalk or limestone, across much of Europe and in England.

Cow Parsnip or Hogweed, *Heracleum sphondylium*, is a large, bristly-hairy perennial plant up to 2m (6ft) tall. Its

Wild Parsnip
Pastinaca sativa

erect stem is hollow and ridged with resin canals in the furrows; its large, pinnate leaves have lobed, serrated leaflets and upper leaves have inflated, sheath-like bases. The flowers vary from greenish-white to pinkish and are borne in large umbels up to 20cm (8in) across, each with 7–10 rays; there are reflexed, linear bracts beneath each partial umbel. Rim flowers have large, notched petals on the outside and smaller inner petals. These large plants are conspicuous in rough grassy places and open woods, roadsides and hedgerows throughout the British Isles and Europe.

Cow Parsnip
Heracleum sphondylium

Upright Hedge-parsley, *Torilis japonica*, grows in hedgerows and grassy places throughout the British Isles and much of Europe, flowering just after Rough Chervil. It is a hairy, annual plant with stiff, erect, ridged stems up to 120cm (4ft) tall and once- to three-times pinnate leaves. The leaflets are lance-shaped and toothed. The white or pinkish flowers grow in compound umbels, each with 5–12 rays and several bracts at the base; they are followed by egg-shaped fruits covered with hooked spines.

Upright Hedge-parsley
Torilis japonica

Wild Carrot, *Daucus carota*, smells like a cultivated carrot but has thin, tough roots. It grows in dry, grassy places and fields, often on calcareous soils and near the sea, throughout the British Isles and Europe. A biennial, it has ferny basal leaves in the first year and flowering stems up to 1m (3ft) tall in the second. Stem leaves are also fern-like, up to three-times pinnate and usually each dense umbel of creamy-white flowers has one central red or purplish flower. Fruiting umbels close up and resemble birds' nests, containing many flattened, spiky fruits.

Wild Carrot
Daucus carota

Heath family

Ericaceae A large family, with about 70 genera and 1500 species, found throughout much of the world, usually in acid soils. All are woody to a greater or lesser extent, and some are large shrubs or trees. There are many fine garden plants among them, including rhododendrons, azaleas and heathers.

Family features Flowers borne singly or in clusters, often showy, usually regular and hermaphrodite. Calyx tubular, formed of 4 or 5 joined sepals; corolla tubular or bell-like, with 4 or 5 joined petals; stamens usually twice as many as petal-lobes; ovary inferior or superior with 4 – 5 cells. Fruits are capsules, berries or drupes. Leaves often evergreen, mostly simple, usually alternate. Stipules 0.

Heather
Calluna vulgaris

Bell-heather
Erica cinerea

Heather or Ling, *Calluna vulgaris*, is the dominant plant on many moors and heaths throughout the British Isles and western Europe, becoming less common further east and south on the Continent. It also grows in open woods. This evergreen shrub grows up to 60cm (2ft) tall, its sprawling branches bearing many leafy side shoots. The small, scale-like leaves are borne in opposite pairs pressed closely to the stems. In late summer Heather plants are transformed by numerous small, bell-like, pinkish-purple flowers; the colour comes from both calyx and corolla.

Bell-heather, *Erica cinerea*, grows on dry heaths and moors throughout the British Isles and western Europe, north to Norway. It is a branched shrub about 60cm (2ft) tall, with many upward-growing stems and numerous leafy side shoots; the leaves are linear with inrolled margins, borne in whorls of three. In late summer the plants flower, transforming the moors (with Heather) into purple instead of dark green. The flowers are reddish-purple, urn-shaped and constricted at the mouth, borne along the tops of the stems.

Cross-leaved Heath, *Erica tetralix*, grows in wetter heaths and moors, bogs and pinewoods throughout the British Isles, western and northern Europe. It is another branched shrub about 60cm (2ft) tall, with more or less upright stems. These bear many linear leaves with margins inrolled almost to the midrib, arranged in cross-like whorls of four (hence Cross-leaved Heath). The rose-pink, urn-shaped flowers appear in late summer in umbel-like clusters nodding at the tops of the stems.

Cross-leaved Heath
Erica tetralix

Five *Vaccinium* species grow in Europe, out of a world total of 150. **Bilberry** or Whortleberry, *V. myrtillus*, forms wide patches of erect stems 30−60cm (1−2ft) tall, with green twigs and ovate, deciduous leaves; in late summer drooping, pink-tinged green, urn-shaped flowers appear in the leaf axils. They are followed by edible blue-black berries. This plant grows in dry, acid soils on mountains, moors and heaths, in open birch and pine woods throughout much of the British Isles and Europe.

Bilberry
Vaccinium myrtillus

Cranberry, *Vaccinium oxycoccus*, is a trailing shrub with slender stems, evergreen, pointed-oblong leaves and nodding, pinkish-white flowers, each with four backward-pointing petals and a cone of fused stamens. The flowers are followed in late summer by edible red berries. This plant grows in bogs, wet heaths and woods across much of Europe and the British Isles.

Cranberry
Vaccinium oxycoccus

Bog Rosemary
Andromeda polifolia

Bearberry
Arctostaphylos uva-ursi

Yellow Bird's-nest
Monotropa hypopitys

Heath family

Bog Rosemary, *Andromeda polifolia*, is an evergreen shrub with spreading stems about 30cm (1ft) tall, narrow leaves and umbel-like clusters of pink or white, bell-shaped flowers in early summer. Plants grow in acid bogs from Wales and northern England into southern Scotland, in central Ireland and across northern Europe, south in the mountains on the Continent.

Bearberry, *Arctostaphylos uva-ursi*, grows on moors and in open woods, often among rocks or on banks, across Europe, in northern England, Scotland and Ireland. It is a prostrate shrub with leathery, spoon-shaped leaves; these are used in herb medicine and for tanning leather. In early summer the plant bears pink-tinged white, bell-like flowers followed by bright red, mealy berries.

Bird's-nest family

Monotropaceae About 12 genera and 30 species in north temperate regions. They are plants without chlorophyll, feeding as saprophytes, growing in soils rich in raw humus, often in coniferous woods. They are white, pink or brownish, their roots covered in mycorrhizal fungi.

Yellow Bird's-nest, *Monotropa hypopitys*, is a waxy-looking plant up to 30cm (1ft) tall, with fleshy stems and alternate, yellowish or ivory-white scale leaves. Each stem is bent over at the top when the flowers are in bud, straightening as the tubular, yellowish bells open. This plant is widespread in Europe, local in England, rare in Wales and Ireland. It grows in beech and pine woods, and on sand-dunes on the coast.

Wintergreen family

Pyrolaceae A small family with 4 genera and about 40 species of evergreen herbs, mostly from Arctic and northern temperate regions. They are partly saprophytic and associated with raw humus, often found in pine woods.

Family features Flowers often nodding, regular and hermaphrodite. Calyx of 4 or 5 fused sepals; petals 5, free; stamens 10; ovary superior with 5 cells. Fruit a capsule. Leaves simple, in basal rosettes, alternate or in whorls. Stipules 0.

Wintergreens, *Pyrola* species, have rosettes of evergreen leaves and erect, leafless flowering stalks with racemes of nodding flowers. There are about five in Europe. **Small Wintergreen**, *P. minor*, is typical, with broadly elliptical leaves and pinkish-white flowers. It usually grows in calcareous soils, in woods, on damp moors and mountain ledges scattered throughout Europe, northern England and Scotland, more rarely in southern England and Ireland.

Small Wintergreen
Pyrola minor

Crowberry family

Empetraceae A very small family, with 3 genera and 9 species from temperate and Arctic regions, South America and Tristan da Cunha.

Crowberry, *Empetrum nigrum*, is the only common member of the family in Europe, found on moors, in birch and pine woods across Europe, in Ireland and northern Britain. It is a low-growing, evergreen plant with slender, sprawling stems and needle-like leaves. Tiny pink flowers grow in the leaf axils, males and females on separate plants; female plants produce black berries.

Crowberry
Empetrum nigrum

Scarlet Pimpernel
Anagallis arvensis

Primrose family

Primulaceae About 20 genera and 1000 species of herbs, mostly found in the northern hemisphere. They include some choice garden plants, such as primroses and cyclamens.

Family features Flowers solitary, or borne in branched clusters or umbels; hermaphrodite and regular. Calyx toothed, formed of 5 fused sepals; corolla lobed, formed of 5 fused petals; stamens 5, opposite the petal-lobes; ovary superior with 1 cell and a single style. Fruit a capsule. Many plants have leaves in basal rosettes. Others have leafy stems with simple or lobed leaves. Stipules 0.

Scarlet Pimpernel, *Anagallis arvensis*, is a little annual plant common throughout Europe and much of the British Isles in gardens and cultivated land, waste places and roadsides, on dunes near the coast. It has sprawling, often prostrate stems with opposite, pointed-ovate leaves; the solitary red flowers open in the morning and close mid-afternoon, remaining closed or closing early in dull weather.

Bog Pimpernel
Anagallis tenella

Bog Pimpernel, *Anagallis tenella*, also has prostrate stems with many opposite, rounded leaves and solitary pink, funnel-shaped flowers in summer. This is a perennial plant, growing in damp, grassy places, in marshes and bogs, wet, open woods and beside pools. It is found in western Europe and scattered throughout many parts of the British Isles, more commonly in the west and absent from much of Scotland.

The **Primulas**, genus *Primula*, are a large group of 500 species centred in Asia and frequently grown in gardens.

Primrose
Primula vulgaris

About 35 are found in Europe.
Primrose, *P. vulgaris*, is one of the
most beloved of spring flowers, nestling
into hedgerows and on shady banks in
woods and meadows, found throughout
much of Europe and the British Isles,
but its numbers have declined in recent
years. This is a perennial plant, with a
clump of wrinkled, lance-shaped leaves
tapering to the base, bright green and
hairless above, paler and hairy on the
underside, growing up to 25cm (10in)
long. In spring the pale yellow, sweet-
scented flowers appear, growing singly
on hairy stalks.

Cowslips, *Primula veris*, bloom a little
later than Primroses in pastures, on
grassy banks and roadsides, usually on
calcareous and base-rich soils. They
grow across Europe, in England and
Wales but are absent from most of
Scotland and found mainly in the centre
of Ireland. Cowslips have wrinkled
leaves, much like those of Primroses,
but the drooping flowers grow in a one-
sided umbel on a much stouter stalk.
They are deeper yellow with orange
spots in the centre, tubular in form with
small lobes around the mouth, sweetly
scented. Hybrids between Cowslips and
Primroses occur where they grow
together, intermediate in form between
the two species. Hybrids between
primroses and oxlips also form.

In Britain, the **Oxlip**, *Primula elatior*, is
found only in eastern England, mainly
in East Anglia, growing in woods in
chalky boulder clay. It is also found in
damp woods and meadows in many
parts of Europe. It has a rosette of
wrinkled leaves and a stout flowering
stalk with a one-sided umbel of pale
yellow flowers, like small, unscented
primroses with orange markings.

Cowslip
Primula veris

Oxlip
Primula elatior

Primrose family

Water Hyacinth, *Hottonia palustris*, is a perennial aquatic species found in ponds, marshes and ditches in many parts of Europe, including England and Wales (mainly in the east). It has floating, much dissected leaves with linear segments, and erect flowering stems up to 40cm (15in) tall in early summer. These bear whorls of lilac, yellow-throated flowers.

Sowbread, *Cyclamen hederifolium*, forms mats of leaves, appearing in late summer after the flowers are over, remaining green through the winter, dying down in spring; they are heart-shaped but with angled edges, with a white margin around a dark green centre, often purplish beneath. The flowers are distinctive, nodding singly on separate stalks, pinkish-purple in colour with reflexed petal-lobes. They are followed by globular capsules with coiled stalks, lying on the ground until they split open to release the seeds just before the new flowers appear. Sowbread grows wild in woods in southern Europe but is planted in gardens elsewhere, including the British Isles, sometimes becoming naturalized. Several other cyclamen species also grow in Europe.

The **Loosestrifes** are a large group of about 200 species in the genus *Lysimachia*, found in many parts of the world. Only nine grow in Europe. **Creeping Jenny**, *L. nummularia*, has prostrate, creeping stems and forms a leafy mat studded with yellow, saucer-shaped flowers around midsummer. The leaves are opposite, rounded and are supposed to resemble pennies. In the wild the plant grows in damp woods

Water Hyacinth
Hottonia palustris

Sowbread
Cyclamen hederifolium

Creeping Jenny
Lysimachia nummularia

and shady hedgebanks, on the edges of streams and ditches throughout Europe and in England and Wales. It is also grown in gardens.

Many *Lysimachia* species are erect plants with leafy stems. **Yellow Loosestrife**, *L. vulgaris*, grows beside rivers and lakes, in fens and marshes, scattered throughout Europe and the British Isles, except the north of Scotland. This perennial plant has leafy stems up to 1.5m (5ft) tall. The leaves are broadly lance-shaped, borne in opposite pairs or in whorls of 3–4, with clusters of yellow, late summer flowers in the axils of the uppermost.

Yellow Loosestrife
Lysimachia vulgaris

Chickweed Wintergreen, *Trientalis europaea*, is a perennial plant with creeping rhizomes and erect stems in spring. Each stem has a whorl of five or six shiny, dark green leaves at the top and one or more white, star-like flowers on long stalks in the centre of the whorl. This attractive plant grows in pine woods and heaths, among moss or in damp grassy places across much of northern Europe, in Scotland and northern England.

Chickweed Wintergreen
Trientalis europaea

Sea Milkwort, *Glaux maritima*, grows in grassy salt marshes, on rocks and cliffs and in estuaries all around the coasts of Europe and the British Isles, also in alkaline places inland. It is a small perennial plant, 30cm (1ft) tall at most, hairless and succulent, with prostrate stems bearing many pairs of pointed-ovate, blue-green leaves. The solitary flowers grow in the leaf axils in summer; they have no petals but the bell-shaped calyx is white or pink and looks like a corolla. The fruits are globular capsules which split into five valves to release the few seeds.

Sea Milkwort
Glaux maritima

Sea Lavender family

Plumbaginaceae A family of herbs and shrubs with 19 genera and 780 species, many associated with the coast and some with mountains. Many grow in the Mediterranean region of Europe and in Asia.

Family features Flowers borne in one-sided inflorescences or heads, with sheathing, often dry, papery bracts; hermaphrodite, regular. Calyx tubular with 5–10 ribs, often papery; petals 5, free or united, often persisting around the fruits; stamens 5, opposite the petals; ovary superior with 1 cell. Fruits dry, often opening by lids. Leaves often in a basal rosette, simple. Stipules 0.

Thrift or Sea Pink, *Armeria maritima*, grows on coastal rocks, on cliffs and in salt marshes on western and northern coasts of Europe and around the British Isles, also in mountains inland. It has been grown in flower gardens for many years. It forms cushions of narrow, rather fleshy leaves growing from the branches of a woody rootstock. In summer the flowers appear — heads of fragrant, red-purple flowers with papery bracts, waving on long stalks.

Thrift
Armeria maritima

Lesser Periwinkle
Vinca minor

Dogbane family

Apocynaceae About 180 genera and over 1500 species of herbs, shrubs and climbing plants, mostly from the tropics and subtropics. Some family members are poisonous, others ornamental; Oleander and Frangipani are both.

Few species are represented in Europe, apart from the five **Periwinkles**, *Vinca* species — trailing or herbaceous plants with funnel-shaped flowers. **Lesser Periwinkle**, *V. minor*, has prostrate stems rooting at the nodes and upright leafy stems little more than 30cm (1ft) tall. They have opposite, evergreen leaves and blue, wheel-like flowers in spring; in southern Europe they are followed by pairs of follicles. Plants grow in woods and hedgerows across much of Europe and Great Britain. A variegated form is grown in gardens.

Bogbean family

Menyanthaceae A small family of aquatic herbs, with 5 genera and 33 species, whose members are found in many parts of the world.

Family features Flowers regular, hermaphrodite. Calyx and corolla both 5-lobed; stamens 5; ovary superior with 1 cell. Fruit a capsule. Leaves alternate, simple or compound.

Bogbean
Menyanthes trifoliata

Bogbean, *Menyanthes trifoliata*, grows beside lakes and ponds, in marshes and bogs, spreading by means of creeping rhizomes and producing many leaves which grow above the surface. Each leaf has three broad leaflets. In early summer the pink-tinged white flowers grow in terminal clusters on separate, leafless stalks; they have delicate, fringed margins to the petals. Bogbean is found throughout the British Isles and Europe.

Fringed Water-lily, *Nymphoides peltata*, looks like a small Water-lily, with floating, heart-shaped leaves on long stalks growing from rhizomes at the bottom of the water. The leaves grow up to 10cm (4in) across and are spotted with purple above, purplish below. The golden-yellow flowers have five fringed petals; they appear in late summer to float on the surface among the leaves.

Fringed Water-lily
Nymphoides peltata

Marsh
Gentian
Gentiana pneumonanthe

Great Yellow Gentian
*Gentiana
lutea*

Felwort
Gentianella amarella

Gentian family

Gentianaceae A family of herbaceous plants with about 80 genera and 900 species, found mostly in temperate regions. Some of the *Gentiana* species are grown in rock gardens.

Family features Flowers regular, hermaphrodite, usually showy. Calyx formed of 4–5 fused sepals; corolla tubular or wheel-shaped, formed of 4–5 brightly coloured, fused petals; stamens as many as and alternating with petal-lobes; ovary superior, usually with 1 cell. Fruit a capsule. Leaves opposite and entire, often connected to each other in pairs across the stem.

About 30 **Gentians** grow in Europe, many in the mountains. Most are perennial plants, often with rosettes of basal leaves and leafy flowering stems. Their flowers are often showy, bright blue or purple. **Marsh Gentian**, *Gentiana pneumonanthe*, has slender stems up to 40cm (15in) tall, linear leaves and blue flowers with green streaks on the outside, borne in a dense cluster at the top of each stem. It grows in wet, acid heaths, marshes and bogs across most of Europe, mainly in southern England in Britain; its numbers are declining.

Some gentians are used in herb medicine, like **Great Yellow Gentian**, *G. lutea*, the source of Gentian Bitter, used to flavour liqueurs and as a tonic for the digestive system. This is a large perennial plant with erect stems up to 2m (6ft) tall and opposite, blue-green leaves, upper ones clasping the stem. In summer dense whorls of yellow flowers grow in the upper leaf axils; each has 5–9 linear petal-lobes forming a star-shaped corolla. Plants grow in damp mountain woods and meadows across much of Europe but are absent from the north and from the British Isles.

The *Gentianella* species are usually annual or biennial plants, often with purple or whitish flowers. **Felwort**, *G. amarella*, is a biennial with a rosette of lance-shaped leaves in the first year and a leafy flowering stem about 30cm (1ft) tall in the second. Its flowers grow in clusters in the upper leaf axils; they are tubular with a fringe of hairs in the throat and may be reddish-purple, blue, pink or white. This little plant grows on basic soils in pastures and short grassland, on sand-dunes and cliffs; it is widespread throughout Europe and many parts of the British Isles, but found less commonly in the west.

Common Centaury
Centaurium erythraea

About 15 **Centauries**, *Centaurium* species, grow in Europe. **Common Centaury**, *C. erythraea*, is typical of many, a biennial plant, with a rosette of elliptical to spoon-shaped leaves in the first year and a flowering stem up to 50cm (20in) tall in the second. This has several pairs of opposite leaves and a branched inflorescence of pink flowers in summer. Plants grow in dry, grassy places, woodland margins and dunes throughout Europe and much of the British Isles.

Yellow-wort, *Blackstonia perfoliata*, is a greyish annual plant with a basal leaf rosette and an erect stem 45cm (18in) tall at most, with opposite leaves fused together around the stem. In summer the yellow flowers appear, their petals widely spreading from a funnel-shaped base. Yellow-wort grows in calcareous soils in short grassland and dunes across most of Europe, except the north, in England, Wales and Ireland.

Yellow-wort
Blackstonia perfoliata

Bedstraw family

Squinancy-wort
Asperula cynanchica

Crosswort
Cruciata laevipes

Rubiaceae Also known as the Madder family. One of the largest families of flowering plants, with about 500 genera and 6000 species of herbs and shrubs, mostly from the tropics. Coffee, quinine and gardenias all come from this family.

Family features Flowers regular, hermaphrodite. Sepals 4−5, free; corolla formed of 4−5 fused petals; stamens as many as and alternating with petal-lobes; ovary inferior, with 2 or more cells. Fruits berries, capsules, or dry and schizocarpic. Leaves simple and usually entire, sometimes toothed, opposite or borne in whorls. Stipules may resemble leaves.

There are not that many members of the family in temperate regions — about 170 in Europe, and the majority of these small, herbaceous plants.
Squinancy-wort, *Asperula cynanchica*, is a small, tufted, grey-green perennial with branched, prostrate non-flowering shoots and erect flowering shoots up to 50cm (20in) tall. Its stems are four-angled and bear whorls of four linear 'leaves', the two true leaves often longer than the others, which are really stipules. The vanilla-scented flowers are borne in clusters at the ends of the flowering shoots; they are funnel-shaped, warty and pale pink outside, white inside. Squinancy-wort grows in dry grassland and dunes on calcareous soils across much of Europe, except the north, in southern England, south Wales and southwestern Ireland.

Crosswort or Mugwort, *Cruciata laevipes*, is a softly hairy, creeping perennial with many weak, four-angled stems branched from the base, growing up to 60cm (2ft) tall. The stems have whorls of four yellow-green, elliptical leaves and clusters of pale yellow, honey-scented flowers in the leaf axils in summer. This little plant grows on calcareous soils, on roadsides and walls, on the sides of chalk pits and in other dry places across much of Europe and Great Britain.

Field Madder, *Sherardia arvensis*, is a small annual plant found as a weed in arable land and waste places, most commonly in dry soils on chalk or limestone. It forms a patch of branched, sprawling stems up to 1m (3ft) across, the stems four-angled with whorls of four leaves on the lower parts, 5–6 on the upper parts. Stem angles and leaves are both rough with tiny prickles. The pale lilac flowers are funnel-shaped, borne in terminal clusters cupped in a ruff of 8–10 lance-shaped bracts like leaves. This plant grows across Europe and much of the British Isles, less commonly in Scotland.

Field Madder
Sherardia arvensis

Wild Madder, *Rubia peregrina*, is a prickly, scrambling plant, a perennial found in hedgerows, woods and scrub near the coasts of western and southern Europe and on British coasts from southern England to Wales and southern Ireland. It has trailing stems up to 120cm (4ft) tall, with prickles on the angles and whorls of 4–6 leaves; these are stiff, shiny dark green, elliptical in shape and prickly on margins and midribs. In summer loose clusters of pale yellow-green flowers appear in the leaf axils and terminating the stems. The fruits are fleshy black berries. Madder, *R. tinctorum*, has been known since prehistoric times as a source of madder dye, used to colour fabrics various shades of red, until replaced by synthetics.

Wild Madder
Rubia peregrina

Bedstraw family

Most of the European members in this family are **Bedstraws**, *Galium* species. They are slender plants, with four-angled, squarish stems and leaves in whorls. Their numerous small flowers are followed by dry, one-seeded nuts borne in pairs.

Lady's
Bedstraw
Galium verum

Heath Bedstraw
Galium saxatile

Lady's Bedstraw, *Galium verum*, was at one time used to stuff mattresses, to curdle milk in cheese-making and in herb medicine. It also yields a red dye. It is a low-growing, perennial plant with wiry, much-branched, creeping stems and upright leafy stems, forming dense patches in short grassland and fixed dunes, along roadsides and hedgebanks throughout Europe and the British Isles. It has whorls of 8–12 leaves on its squarish stems and dense clusters of yellow flowers in late summer.

Many bedstraws are similar to Lady's Bedstraw, but the majority have white flowers, like **Heath Bedstraw**, *Galium saxatile*. This plant forms a mat of prostrate non-flowering stems, all with ovate leaves in whorls of 6–8. In summer the upright flowering shoots grow about 10–20cm (4–8in) tall, with narrower leaves and clusters of white flowers. The plant becomes black when dried. It grows in acid soils, on heaths and moors, grassland and scrub throughout most of Europe and the British Isles.

Hedge Bedstraw, *Galium mollugo,* is a taller, almost scrambling plant, often found at the base of a hedgebank, but also in woods and waste places, rough grassland and scrub, on calcareous soils throughout much of Europe and the British Isles. It is a perennial with

Hedge Bedstraw
Galium mollugo

numerous, branched, weak stems, many whorls of 6−8 oblong to elliptical leaves and loose, branched clusters of flowers in the latter half of summer. It does not turn black on drying.

Marsh Bedstraw, *Galium palustre*, is a variable, straggling, much-branched plant 30−120cm (1−4ft) tall, often with weak stems, rough on the angles and blackening when dried. It has whorls of 4−6 elliptical or oblong leaves and white flowers borne in loose clusters terminating the stems. This plant grows in wet meadows and fens throughout the British Isles and Europe.

Marsh Bedstraw
Galium
palustre

Cleavers or Goosegrass, *Galium aparine*, is an annual plant with weak, scrambling, angled stems growing up to 120cm (4ft) tall and clinging to vegetation by hooked bristles on the angles. The narrow leaves grow in whorls of 6−8 and small clusters of tiny, greenish-white flowers grow in the leaf axils. The pairs of globular fruits that follow are covered in tiny hooks. Plants grow in damp, shady places all over Europe and the British Isles. Their fruits can be roasted as a coffee substitute and young shoots can be eaten as a green vegetable or in salads. Cleavers is also used in herb medicine for purifying the blood.

Cleavers
Galium aparine

Sweet Woodruff, *Galium odoratum*, is a perennial, carpeting plant found in damp, shady woods on base-rich soils throughout Europe and the British Isles. It forms erect, unbranched stems, 45cm (18in) tall at most, each with several whorls of 6−8 firm, lance-shaped leaves and a branched cluster of white flowers at the top. The whole plant has the scent of new-mown hay, retaining its fragrance when dried.

Sweet Woodruff
Galium odoratum

Phlox family

Polemoniaceae A small family with about 15 genera and 300 species, mostly herbs from western North America. Phloxes are grown in gardens.

One of the few representatives of this family in Europe is **Jacob's Ladder**, *Polemonium caeruleum*, a perennial plant with a clump of erect stems up to 90cm (3ft) tall and alternate, pinnate leaves. The leaves are large, with 6–12 pairs of pointed-elliptical leaflets and one terminal leaflet. Showy blue flowers grow at the tops of the stems; each has a funnel-shaped corolla with five petal-lobes in a five-toothed calyx. Plants grow in damp mountain woods and pastures in northern and central Europe, also in a few places on limestone hills in northern England.

Jacob's Ladder
Polemonium caeruleum

Bindweed family

Convolvulaceae A mostly tropical family, with about 55 genera and 1650 species of herbs and shrubs, many of them climbers. Morning glories and sweet potatoes come from this family.

  Family features Flowers regular, hermaphrodite. Sepals 5, free, often overlapping; corolla funnel-shaped, formed of 5 fused petals; stamens 5, alternating with petal-lobes; ovary superior with 1–4 cells. Fruits usually capsules. Leaves simple, alternate. Stipules 0. Stems contain milky juice.

Field Bindweed, *Convolvulus arvensis*, grows in cultivated and waste land, on roadsides, in short grassland and near the sea throughout Europe, England and Wales, less commonly in Ireland, rarely in Scotland. This perennial weed has underground rhizomes which

Field Bindweed
Convolvulus arvensis

penetrate to a depth of 2m (6ft) or more, so that they are difficult to eradicate. Its stems twist anticlockwise around fences and plants, strangling them if left alone. They bear arrow-shaped leaves and white or pink flowers which are funnel-shaped.

Hedge Bindweed, *Calystegia sepium*, is a similar but larger plant, with arrow-shaped leaves 5–15cm (2–5in) long and funnel-shaped flowers about 6cm (3in) across. Its flowers tend to be white but may be pink. This is another strangler with twining stems, but as it is bigger it can do more damage, swamping surrounding plants with its foliage. It grows in waste places, woodland margins and hedges, in gardens and on roadsides throughout Europe and the British Isles, less commonly in Scotland.

Hedge Bindweed
Calystegia sepium

Sea Bindweed, *Calystegia soldanella*, grows on shores, sand-dunes and shingle along the Atlantic and Mediterranean coasts of Europe, all around the British Isles. It has penetrating rhizomes and spreading, sprawling stems with fleshy, kidney-shaped leaves on long stalks. In summer large, pink or purple flowers appear in the leaf axils.

Sea Bindweed
Calystegia soldanella

The **Dodders**, *Cuscuta* species, are parasitic plants without roots but with yellow or brown twining stems, leaves reduced to tiny scales and clusters of small flowers in late summer. About 15 species grow in Europe. **Common Dodder**, *C. epithymum*, is found across most of the Continent, mainly in southern England in the British Isles, most often on gorse and heathers. It may also grow on crops like clovers and alfalfa. Its red, thread-like stems bear dense clusters of scented, pink flowers in summer.

Common Dodder
Cuscuta epithymum

Houndstongue
Cynoglossum officinale

Common Comfrey
Symphytum officinale

Tuberous Comfrey
Symphytum tuberosum

Forget-me-not family

Boraginaceae About 100 genera and 2000 species of herbs from temperate and tropical areas, especially from the Mediterranean region and eastern Asia. Ornamental plants in the family include pulmonarias and forget-me-nots. Several species, like Comfrey and Borage, are used in herb medicine.

Family features Flowers borne in coiled, one-sided clusters which uncurl as they open; hermaphrodite, regular. Calyx formed of 5 fused sepals; corolla lobed, formed of 5 fused petals; stamens 5, alternating with the petal-lobes; ovary superior with 2 or 4 cells, entire or 4-lobed with the style protruding from the middle of the lobes. Fruit consists of 4 nutlets. Leaves simple, usually alternate. Stipules 0. Plants are often coarsely hairy.

Houndstongue, *Cynoglossum officinale*, grows in dry, grassy places and woodland margins across much of Europe and the British Isles, often on fixed dunes and in sandy places near the sea. This is a biennial plant, with a clump of large, broadly lance-shaped basal leaves and erect, leafy stems up to 90cm (3ft) tall, all covered with soft grey hairs. Its stems end in curled clusters of dull red, funnel-shaped flowers, followed by nutlets covered with barbed spines.

Common Comfrey, *Symphytum officinale*, is one of 12 *Symphytum* species found in Europe. It is a coarse perennial plant with clumps of large, bristly stems and leaves, the stems growing up to 120cm (4ft) tall and ending in coiled clusters of tubular, yellowish-white, pinkish or blue flowers in early summer. The bases of the leaves run down the stems, making them appear winged. This plant grows in damp places, on riverbanks, in ditches and wet meadows across much of Europe and the British Isles. It has a long history of use in herb medicine, especially for healing wounds, sprains and broken bones (hence its other names of Knitbone and Boneset).

Tuberous Comfrey, *Symphytum tuberosum*, is a similar but smaller plant, 50cm (20in) tall at most, with thick, creeping rhizomes, unbranched stems and large, elliptical leaves halfway up the stems. The flowers are yellowish-white. It grows in damp woods and hedges, in wet meadows and beside streams across most of Europe and scattered in Great Britain.

Lungwort
Pulmonaria officinalis

Lungwort, *Pulmonaria officinalis*, is widely grown in gardens for its clumps of white-spotted, heart-shaped or ovate leaves and early spring flowers borne in clusters on short, erect stalks. The flowers open pink from pink buds and then turn blue. Lungwort also grows wild across much of Europe in woods and hedgerows, in scattered places in Great Britain, probably growing as a garden escape in many areas.

Green Alkanet, *Pentaglottis sempervirens*, is a bristly perennial plant with a clump of pointed-oval leaves and several erect, leafy flowering stems ending in curled clusters of bright blue flowers in early summer. Each flower is tubular with spreading petal-lobes and white scales in the centre, closing the throat. Plants grow in woods, hedgerows and damp shady places in western Europe and Great Britain.

Green Alkanet
Pentaglottis sempervirens

Forget-me-not family

Blue-eyed Mary
Omphalodes verna

Blue-eyed Mary, *Omphalodes verna*, is a perennial plant with long, prostrate stems and low carpets of ovate or heart-shaped leaves on long stalks. Racemes of sky blue flowers appear on leafy stalks in spring. This little plant grows wild in woods of western and southern Europe, and is also grown in gardens elsewhere, including parts of Britain.

Alkanet, *Anchusa officinalis*, is a bristly perennial plant, its leafy stems growing up to 90cm (3ft) tall, bearing long, lance-shaped leaves and ending in coiled clusters of funnel-shaped flowers. These open red and turn blue as they age. Plants grow in meadows and arable land, in waste places and on roadsides throughout continental Europe, only as a casual in southern England in the British Isles.

Alkanet
Anchusa officinalis

Bugloss, *Anchusa arvensis*, is a very bristly annual or biennial plant, with stems 15–20cm (6–8in) tall and lance-shaped, wavy-margined leaves, upper ones clasping the stems. The bright blue flowers are borne in branched inflorescences at the top of the stems; each one has five white, hairy scales at the centre. This little plant grows in arable land and heaths, especially on sandy or chalky soils, and near the sea; it is found throughout Europe and much of Great Britain, also on the eastern and northern coasts of Ireland.

Bugloss
Anchusa arvensis

The **Forget-me-nots**, *Myosotis* species, are probably the most familiar plants in this family; there are about 20 species in Europe. Cultivated varieties of the Wood Forget-me-not, *M. sylvatica*, are those grown in gardens, but plants also grow wild throughout Europe, in woods and damp meadows, mainly in England and southern Scotland in the British Isles and rarely in the west. It has a rosette of hairy, ovate or spoon-shaped leaves and branched flowering stems in spring, up to 45cm (18in) tall. As in all forget-me-nots, the flower clusters are coiled at first, unfurling as the bright blue flowers gradually open.

Water Foget-me-not
Myosotis scorpioides

Water Forget-me-not, *Myosotis scorpioides*, grows in wet places and in water, beside streams and ponds, in marshes and wet meadows throughout Europe and the British Isles. This is a perennial plant with leafy stems which creep a little and then turn upwards to unfurl coiled clusters of sky blue, yellow-eyed flowers. It is a sprawling plant, 60cm (2ft) tall at most.

Field Forget-me-not, *Myosotis arvensis*, has smaller flowers than either of the former species, the corolla only 3mm (⅛in) across. It is like a small Wood Forget-me-not, with a rosette of elliptical leaves and erect, leafy stems up to 30cm (1ft) tall, bearing coiled clusters of grey-blue flowers at the top. It grows on roadsides and on cultivated ground, also on dunes, throughout Europe and the British Isles.

Field
Forget-me-not
Myosotis arvensis

Changing Forget-me-not, *Myosotis discolor*, gets its name from its flowers — they open creamy-white, then change colour to pink and blue. This is a small annual plant, with a rosette of hairy, lance-shaped leaves and slender, leafy stems up to 30cm (1ft) tall, ending in coiled clusters of the very small, changing flowers. It grows in grassy places on light soils throughout Europe and the British Isles.

Changing
Forget-me-not
Myosotis discolor

Forget-me-not family

Common Gromwell
Lithospermum officinale

Gromwell is a name given to several *Lithospermum* species, of which there are about 17 in Europe. **Common Gromwell**, *L. officinale*, is a rather bristly, perennial plant with much-branched, leafy stems growing up to 80cm (30in) tall; many coiled clusters of yellowish-white flowers grow in the leaf axils and at the tops of the branches. The clusters lengthen and straighten as they age. This plant grows in hedgerows and woodland margins throughout Europe, mainly in England in the British Isles.

Corn Gromwell, *Lithospermum arvense*, is a weed of arable land found throughout Europe, mainly in England in the British Isles. It is a rather bristly annual plant with a little-branched, erect stem, usually about 50cm (20in) tall at most. It has many leaves, the lower ones bluntly oblong and the upper ones linear and stalkless. Leafy clusters of small white flowers terminate the stems in early summer.

Corn Gromwell
Lithospermum arvense

Oyster Plant, *Mertensia maritima*, in contrast to many members of this family, is hairless and rather fleshy, an adaptation to its life on the sea shore. It grows on sand and shingle beaches on the Atlantic coast of Europe from Jutland northwards, and on the northern coasts of England, Scotland and northern Ireland, but is rare everywhere and decreasing. It forms a mat of sprawling stems with two rows of opposite, blue-grey, spoon-shaped leaves and clusters of funnel-shaped flowers in summer; they are pink at first, soon turning blue and pink.

Oyster Plant
Mertensia maritima

Viper's Bugloss, *Echium vulgare*, is almost prickly, with very large, bristly hairs. This biennial plant has a rosette of large, lance-shaped leaves in the first year and a leafy flowering stem up to 90cm (3ft) tall in the second. The flowers grow in coiled clusters in the axils of the upper leaves, pink in bud, opening bright blue and funnel-shaped; each has four or five long, protruding stamens. Plants grow in dry soils, waste ground and grassy places, on cliffs near the sea and on sand-dunes throughout Europe and much of England and Wales, rarely in Scotland, on the east coast in Ireland.

Vervain family

Viper's Bugloss
Echium vulgare

Verbenaceae A mainly tropical and subtropical family, with about 75 genera and 3000 species of herbs, shrubs and trees. Verbenas and Lemon Verbena are grown in gardens. Teak comes from an Asian tree in this family.

Of the few representatives of this family in Europe, most are shrubs. However, **Vervain**, *Verbena officinalis*, is a perennial plant growing 30–75cm (12–30in) tall, with stiffly branched, four-angled stems resembling a candelabrum, and rough, opposite, pinnately cut leaves. Its pale lilac flowers are borne in long, terminal spikes and open a few at a time in late summer; individually they are small and tubular with five petal-lobes. Each flower is followed by four reddish-brown nutlets. Vervain grows in waste places and on roadsides throughout much of Europe, except the north, mainly in England, Wales and southern Ireland in the British Isles. It is well known in herb medicine as a cold and fever remedy.

Vervain
Verbena officinalis

Nightshade family

Solanaceae About 90 genera and 2000 species, mostly herbs and twining plants, many from warmer parts of the world, especially Central and South America. Food plants in the family include potatoes, tomatoes and peppers. Some species are poisonous, including Belladonna, Henbane and the tobaccos.

Family features Flowers solitary or borne in cymes, usually hermaphrodite, regular. Calyx has 3–6 (usually 5) lobes, persistent; corolla has 5 lobes; stamens alternate with corolla lobes; ovary superior with 2 cells. Fruit a berry or capsule. Leaves alternate, simple. Stipules 0.

Belladonna
Atropa belladonna

Black Nightshade
Solanum nigrum

Woody Nightshade
Solanum dulcamara

Belladonna, *Atropa belladonna*, is one of the most poisonous plants known. It is a glandular perennial, with branched, leafy stems 1.5m (5ft) or more tall and large, pointed-ovate leaves. In summer bell-shaped, violet-brown flowers droop from the leaf axils, followed by berries, green at first, ripening glossy black. Plants grow in calcareous soils in hedgerows and woods across most of Europe, relatively rarely in the British Isles, mainly in England and Wales.

Nightshades are a large group of about 1500 *Solanum* species, mainly from the tropics; few grow in Europe. **Black Nightshade**, *S. nigrum*, is a weed of gardens and waste places, cultivated land and vineyards in many parts of Europe, mainly in England and Wales in the British Isles. It is a leafy annual, with branched green stems up to 60cm (2ft) tall, irregularly toothed leaves, clusters of white flowers and black berries. The stamens of nightshades are characteristic, with short filaments and large, protruding yellow anthers.

The branched, scrambling stems of
Woody Nightshade or Bittersweet,
Solanum dulcamara, often grow 2m (6ft)
tall in waste places, woodland margins
and hedgerows, in shingle or on dunes
near the sea. The plant is found
throughout Europe and the British
Isles, rarely in Scotland and Ireland. It
has simple or lobed leaves, racemes of
blue-purple flowers with reflexed petal-
lobes and yellow anthers, and clusters of
berries, green at first and ripening red.
Like those of many nightshades, the
berries are dangerous to children.

Thorn-apple
Datura stramonium

Thorn-apple, *Datura stramonium*, is a
very poisonous plant with the same
poisons as Belladonna – the alkaloids
atropine and hyoscyamine. It is a
coarse, hairless annual with a foetid
scent, a branched, often purplish stem
up to 2m (6ft) tall and large, coarsely
toothed leaves. Its solitary flowers have
an elongated, winged calyx and funnel-
shaped, white corolla. The fruits are
prickly capsules containing rough, black
seeds. This plant grows in waste places,
cultivated land and riverine sandbanks
across much of Europe; it is an
uncommon casual of waste ground in
Great Britain.

Henbane
Hyoscyamus niger

Henbane, *Hyoscyamus niger*, contains
the same poisons as Thorn-apple and
also has an unpleasant scent. It is a
coarse annual or biennial plant, stickily
hairy, with branched, leafy stems up to
80cm (30in) tall; the leaves are lobed or
coarsely toothed. The flowers are
funnel-shaped, greenish-yellow with
purple veins, borne in one-sided clusters
in late summer and followed by capsules
enclosed in calyces. Plants grow in
disturbed places, often in sandy soils,
around farms or near the sea throughout
Europe and the British Isles.

Mint family

Labiatae or **Lamiaceae**. About 180 genera and 3500 species of herbs and shrubs found in much of the world, many in the Mediterranean area. Plants like mint, sage and rosemary are kitchen herbs; others, like peppermint, are medicinal herbs. Bergamot is used to flavour Earl Grey tea, and rosemary, balm and peppermint in liqueurs. Lavender is used in the perfume industry. Garden plants include salvias, lavender and catmint.

Family features Flowers often in spikes, made up of whorls of flowers in the axils of bracts, hermaphrodite and bilaterally symmetrical. Calyx tubular with 5 teeth; corolla tubular, 5-lobed, often 2-lipped; stamens 2 or 4; ovary superior with 2 deeply lobed cells and a style in the cleft in the centre. Fruit consists of 4 nutlets. Stem usually square. Leaves opposite. Stipules 0. Many species contain aromatic oils.

There are about 20 **Mints**, *Mentha* species, in Europe, all more or less scented plants with small, weakly two-lipped flowers in shades of lilac or white, each one with four petal-lobes.

Water Mint, *Mentha aquatica*, is common throughout Europe and the British Isles beside water, in marshes and wet woods. It is a perennial with a strong spearmint scent, erect, branched stems up to 90cm (3ft) tall and pointed-ovate, serrated leaves on long stalks. The lilac flowers appear in late summer, borne at the tops of the stems in dense, oblong heads, often broken into whorls.

Spearmint, *Mentha spicata*, grows in damp places, beside roads and in waste ground in much of Europe and the

Water Mint
Mentha aquatica

Spearmint
Mentha spicata

British Isles. It is also grown in gardens and made into mint sauce. This perennial plant has stems up 90cm (3ft) tall, serrated, lance-shaped leaves and an unmistakable scent. In late summer each stem bears whorls of pink or lilac flowers. Peppermint, *Mentha x piperita*, is a hybrid between Spearmint and Water Mint; it grows wild in damp places and is also cultivated for its Oil of Peppermint, used to flavour sweets, liqueurs, medicines and toothpaste.

Corn Mint
Mentha arvensis

Corn Mint, *Mentha arvensis*, is a perennial plant with a rather sickly scent, erect stems up to 60cm (2ft) tall and toothed, ovate or elliptical leaves. Its lilac or white flowers grow in dense whorls in the axils of the upper leaves. Plants grow in damp places, in grassy openings in woods, in meadows and arable fields throughout most of Europe and the British Isles.

Pennyroyal
Mentha pulegium

Pennyroyal, *Mentha pulegium*, has prostrate stems with opposite, ovate leaves and flowering stems up to 30cm (1ft) tall in late summer, with dense whorls of lilac flowers in the upper leaf axils. The whole plant smells of peppermint. It grows in wet, grassy places, beside ponds and streams across Europe, except the north, mainly in England and Wales in Britain.

Gipsywort, *Lycopus europaeus*, is a perennial plant with erect, leafy stems up to 1m (3ft) tall, much branched with opposite, pinnately lobed, elliptical leaves. Its white flowers grow in dense whorls in axils of the upper leaves in summer; each one is tubular with four lobes. This plant grows in marshes and wet woods, beside rivers and ditches throughout Europe and much of the British Isles. It yields a black dye.

Gipsywort
Lycopus europaeus

Mint family

One of the best known kitchen herbs in this family is **Wild Marjoram** or Oregano, *Origanum vulgare*, found wild all over Europe and much of the British Isles. It favours calcareous soils, dry, grassy places, hedgebanks, roadsides or scrub, forming patches of erect, purplish stems about 60cm (2ft) tall with opposite, ovate leaves and the characteristic marjoram scent. In late summer the flowers appear — dense, rounded clusters of reddish-purple to pale pink, two-lipped flowers growing on long stalks in the leaf axils and at the tops of the stems.

Wild
Marjoram
Origanum vulgare

Wild Thyme, *Thymus praecox*, is a small, matted perennial plant, with branched, prostrate stems and small, elliptical leaves. In summer the plants produce rows of side stems along the main shoots, each with a terminal head of small, purple, two-lipped flowers. This plant grows in dry, grassy places, on downs and heaths, banks and screes, sometimes in fixed dunes, throughout Europe and much of the British Isles. It has a scent similar to, but weaker than, the related Garden Thyme, *T. vulgaris*.

Wild Thyme
Thymus praecox

Wild Basil, *Clinopodium vulgare*, is a rather straggling perennial plant with a faint aromatic scent. It has erect stems up to 80cm (30in) tall and opposite, ovate leaves with serrated margins. The flowers are two-lipped, pinkish-purple and borne in dense whorls in the upper leaf axils in late summer. They fall to leave hairy, purplish calyces containing the nutlets. This plant grows in dry, usually calcareous soils, in hedgebanks and scrub on rocky banks and slopes throughout Europe and much of Great Britain, rarely in Ireland.

Wild Basil
Clinopodium vulgare

About 700 species of **Sage** grow in the warmer temperate and tropical regions of the world, all belonging to the genus *Salvia*. They are a variable group of small shrubs and herbaceous plants, often aromatic; some are grown as ornamentals in gardens, a few are used in herb medicine and as kitchen herbs. About 45 grow in Europe, the majority in the Mediterranean region, like culinary Sage, *S. officinalis*.

Meadow Clary, *Salvia pratensis*, grows in meadows and other grassy places, usually on calcareous soils, throughout much of Europe, locally in England. It is a perennial plant with a clump of oblong, heart-shaped leaves, long-stalked, rather wrinkled and with serrated margins. In summer the leafy flowering stems grow up to 1m (3ft) tall and bear whorls of flowers in toothed, hairy calyces. The flowers are tubular and two-lipped, with a curved, hooded upper lip; two stamens and/or the style protrude from beneath the hood (this kind of flower is typical of many sage species). The flowers are violet-blue and may be larger and hermaphrodite or smaller and female, usually the two kinds on separate plants.

Meadow Clary
Salvia pratensis

Wild Clary, *Salvia verbenaca*, is a smaller plant, 80cm (30in) tall at most, often tinged with blue-purple at the tops of the stems and with deeply toothed, almost lobed leaves. Its flowers are blue or lilac with two white spots at the base of the lower lip, either female or hermaphrodite. Many of them never open but are self-pollinated. This plant grows in dry grassland and roadsides, sometimes in sand-dunes, throughout much of Mediterranean and western Europe; in Britain it is found mainly in southern and eastern England.

Wild Clary
Salvia verbenaca

Mint family

Self-heal, *Prunella vulgaris*, is found throughout Europe and the British Isles, a common plant of waste and grassy places, gardens and roadsides, pastures and open woods. It is a small perennial with erect stems up to 50cm (20in) tall and ovate or lance-shaped, sometimes toothed, leaves. In summer its blue-violet, two-lipped flowers appear, borne in dense clusters amidst hairy bracts at the tops of the stems.

Self-heal
Prunella vulgaris

The **Woundworts** are a large group of about 300 species in the genus *Stachys*, found throughout the world, with about 65 in Europe. They have leafy, erect stems and whorls of flowers in the upper leaf axils, the whole forming a spike-like inflorescence. The flowers are two-lipped, the lower lip three-lobed and the upper lip flat or hooded.

Betony, *Stachys officinalis*, is a perennial plant with a clump of wrinkled basal leaves — long-stalked with oblong blades and toothed margins. The erect flowering stalks, almost leafless, grow in summer to about 60cm (2ft) tall and bear many whorls of bright reddish-purple flowers with toothed calyces, the lower whorls often separated from each other. This plant grows in open woods and hedge, grassland and heaths, usually in light soils, throughout most of Europe north to southern Sweden, in England and Wales, rarely in Scotland and Ireland. In the past it was used in herb medicine to cure headaches or made into poultices to treat cuts and bruises.

Betony
Stachys officinalis

Hedge Woundwort, *Stachys sylvatica*, has long green rhizomes and leafy stems growing up to 1m (3ft) tall. Rhizome

Hedge Woundwort
Stachys sylvatica

and leaves both have an unpleasant scent if bruised. The stems are glandular-hairy, the leaves heart-shaped with serrated margins and long stalks. In late summer the flowers form spikes at the ends of the stems, growing in well-separated whorls in the axils of bracts; they are dull reddish-purple with white markings. This perennial plant grows in shady places, woods and hedgebanks throughout Europe and the British Isles. It has antiseptic properties and at one time its leaves were made into poultices to bind around wounds.

Marsh Woundwort
Stachys palustris

Marsh Woundwort, *Stachys palustris*, was used in the same ways. It is similar to Hedge Woundwort but almost odourless; its rhizomes produce small tubers at the ends and its leaves are lance-shaped. Its late-summer flowers are dull purple with white markings. Marsh Woundwort grows in wet places, in marshes and fens, beside streams and ponds throughout Europe and the British Isles, but is absent from parts of the north.

Field Woundwort, *Stachys arvensis*, is a little, annual plant with a clump of slender, branched stems only 25cm (10in) tall at most. They are leafy, with long-stalked, ovate or heart-shaped leaves, wavy-margined or toothed and hairy like the stalks. The flowers are pale purple, borne in whorls in the axils of bracts, forming a very loose, interrupted spike at the tops of the stems; plants can be found in flower for much of the year. This little plant grows in acid soils in lowland areas, often in sandy arable fields; it is found throughout Europe and much of Great Britain but is absent from many parts of northern England and Scotland, scattered in Ireland.

Field Woundwort
Stachys arvensis

White Deadnettle
Lamium album

Red Deadnettle
Lamium purpureum

Henbit
Lamium amplexicaule

Mint family

The **Deadnettles** are a group of about 40 *Lamium* species from Europe and Asia. They have leafy stems and dense whorls of flowers in the axils of leafy bracts high up on the stems; the flowers are two-lipped, with a hooded upper lip and a three-lobed lower lip in which the two lateral lobes are very small.

White Deadnettle, *Lamium album*, is found across most of Europe and much of the British Isles in grassy hedgebanks, along roadsides and in waste places. This small, hairy, perennial plant has a clump of erect stems up to 60cm (2ft) tall and opposite coarsely toothed and heart-shaped leaves. The whorls of white flowers grow at the tops of the stems in the axils of purple-tinged, leaf-like bracts. Plants bloom from spring to autumn, but when not in flower they may be mistaken for Stinging Nettle — all they lack is the sting.

Red Deadnettle, *Lamium purpureum*, is a weedy annual plant with a pungent scent when bruised, growing in waste places and cultivated ground throughout the British Isles and Europe. It forms a small clump of branched stems with heart-shaped, long-stalked leaves, stems and leaves hairy and often purple-tinged. Plants bloom from early spring to late autumn; the flowers are pinkish-purple, borne with purple bracts in dense whorls near the top of each stem.

Henbit, *Lamium amplexicaule*, is an annual plant with branched, rather sprawling stems up to 25cm (10in) tall and scalloped, rounded leaves, the upper ones clasping the stem. In summer a few whorls of pinkish-purple flowers grow in the axils of bracts at the tops of the stems. Henbit grows in light, cultivated soils, in arable land and waste places throughout Europe and most of the British Isles.

Yellow Archangel, *Lamiastrum galeobdolon*, forms large patches of erect, leafy stems up to 60cm (2ft) tall with pointed-oval, coarsely toothed leaves. In summer its showy yellow flowers appear in the axils of leaf-like bracts at the tops of the stems; each has a helmet-shaped upper lip and a three-lobed lower lip marked with red-brown streaks. This plant grows in heavy soils, in woods and other shady places throughout Europe, England and Wales, rarely in Scotland and Ireland.

Yellow
Archangel
*Lamiastrum
galeobdolon*

There are about 10 **Hempnettles**, *Galeopsis* species, nine found in Europe. Like all of them, **Common Hempnettle**, *G. tetrahit*, is an annual plant with two-lipped flowers borne in dense whorls in the axils of bracts at the tops of the stems. The flowers grow in spiny-toothed calyces. This is a roughly hairy plant, with erect, branched stems up to 1m (3ft) tall and coarse, toothed leaves like those of nettles but without the stinging hairs. The stems are swollen and especially hairy just below the nodes. The flowers are pink or purple with darker markings. This plant grows in damp arable land, in marshes and fens throughout Europe and the British Isles.

Common Hempnettle
Galeopsis tetrahit

Large-flowered Hempnettle, *Galeopsis speciosa*, is like Common Hempnettle but has much larger yellow flowers, often with a purple blotch on the lower lip. It grows in arable land, often in peaty soils, across much of Europe, scattered throughout much of the British Isles.

Large-flowered Hempnettle
Galeopsis speciosa

Motherwort
Leonurus cardiaca

Black
Horehound
Ballota nigra

Catmint
Nepeta cataria

Mint family

Motherwort, *Leonurus cardiaca*, is an old medicinal plant used to treat nervous and heart disorders. It grows in waste places, in hedgebanks and beside roads across much of central Europe, but is a rare introduction in the British Isles, found only in England. This perennial plant has branched stems 60–120cm (2–4ft) tall and long-stalked, palmately lobed leaves; they have a pungent scent if bruised. The lower leaves have 5–7 irregularly toothed lobes and the upper ones have three pointed lobes. The flowers appear in late summer, borne in whorls in the axils of three-lobed bracts at the tops of the stems; they are pink and two-lipped, with a white-bearded upper lip, and spine-tipped calyx-lobes.

Black Horehound, *Ballota nigra*, has a disagreeable scent, dark green leaves and dull purple flowers in summer. It grows on roadsides and in hedgebanks across most of Europe and England, more locally in Wales, rarely in Scotland and Ireland. It is a hairy perennial, with branched stems, toothed, ovate leaves and whorls of two-lipped flowers in the axils of leaf-like bracts.

Catmint, *Nepeta cataria*, grows wild in hedgebanks and on roadsides throughout Europe, scattered in England, Wales and Ireland, only in the south in Scotland. It is also grown in gardens where cats love its distinctive scent. This is a perennial plant forming a patch of more or less erect stems up to 1m (3ft) tall, with toothed, ovate leaves whitened by soft, dense hairs. In late summer clusters of red-spotted white, two-lipped flowers grow in the axils of the upper leaves and terminating the stems.

At one time **Ground Ivy**, *Glechoma hederacea*, was called Alehoof, since it was used to give the bitter taste to beer. This perennial plant has creeping stems up to 60cm (2ft) long and rounded heart-shaped leaves with wavy margins. In spring and early summer its stems turn upwards to bear blue-purple, two-lipped flowers in twos or fours in the leaf axils. It grows in damp places, often in heavy soils, in woods and hedgebanks, waste places and grassland throughout Europe and the British Isles, rarely in northern Scotland.

Ground Ivy
Glechoma hederacea

White Horehound, *Marrubium vulgare*, is a medicinal plant used to treat coughs and bronchitis. It is an aromatic perennial with branched, erect stems 30−60cm (2−3ft) tall and wrinkled, ovate leaves all covered with woolly white hairs. In summer dense whorls of white, two-lipped flowers appear in the upper leaf axils; each has a notched upper lip and a three-lobed lower lip. Plants grow in dry, open places, waste ground, dry, grassy slopes and downs, and on roadsides throughout much of Europe, scattered in England and Wales, rarely in Scotland and Ireland.

White Horehound
Marrubium vulgare

About 12 **Skullcaps**, *Scutellaria* species, grow in Europe. They are perennial plants, with simple leaves and two-lipped, frequently S-shaped flowers. **Skullcap**, *S. galericulata*, forms patches of erect, often branched stems up to 50cm (20in) tall, with toothed, lance-shaped leaves and bright blue flowers in the axils of bracts at the tops of the stems; the flowers may be solitary or borne in pairs. This plant grows in wet meadows and fens, in marshes and beside rivers and ponds throughout Europe and the British Isles.

Skullcap
Scutellaria galericulata

Mint family

Wood Sage
Teucrium scorodonia

Germanders are a group of about 300 *Teucrium* species found worldwide with about 50 in Europe. Their flowers are distinctive, with a corolla that lacks an upper lip, but has a five-lobed lower lip, the central lobe the largest and often hanging. **Wood Sage**, *T. scorodonia*, grows in heaths and woods, usually in dry, non-calcareous soils, sometimes on dunes or shingle, in western and central Europe and much of Great Britain, in all but central Ireland. It is a perennial plant, with branched stems, rounded, wrinkled, sage-green leaves and spikes of pale yellowish-green flowers up to 60cm (2ft) tall.

Bugle, *Ajuga reptans*, is a perennial plant, with leafy, prostrate stems and rosettes of smooth, ovate leaves often tinged with bronze. In summer the flowering stems grow up to 30cm (1ft) tall, each with a terminal, leafy inflorescence formed of many whorls of blue flowers. Each flower has a short upper lip and a three-lobed lower lip. Plants grow in damp woods and meadows throughout Europe and the British Isles. They are also grown in damp places in gardens.

Bugle
Ajuga reptans

Figwort family

Scrophulariaceae Over 200 genera and nearly 3000 species of herbs and shrubs found almost worldwide. Many have showy flowers; some, like veronicas, penstemons and antirrhinums, are grown in gardens.

 Family features Flowers usually bilaterally symmetrical, hermaphrodite. Calyx 5-lobed; corolla lobed or 2-lipped, formed of 4–5 fused petals; stamens usually 2 or 4, inserted in pairs on the corolla (if a fifth stamen is present it is usually different and sterile); ovary superior with 2 cells. Fruits are capsules or, rarely, berries. Leaves simple or pinnate. Stipules 0.

The **Mulleins**, *Verbascum* species, are usually biennial plants, forming a rosette of leaves in the first year and a tall flowering stem in the second, with a spike of many flowers. Several are grown in gardens. **Great Mullein** or Aaron's Rod, *V. thapsus*, grows on sunny banks and roadsides, in waste places and rough grassland, usually in dry soils, throughout Europe and the British Isles. The stout 2-m (6-ft) tall flowering stem bears grey-woolly leaves, arranged to direct water down the stem to the roots, and many yellow flowers.

White Mullein, *Verbascum lychnitis*, has grey woolly stems and dense white hairs beneath the lance-shaped leaves; the upper leaf surfaces are green. It is a biennial with a branched flowering stem up to 1.5m (5ft) tall in the second year and white flowers. Plants grow in waste places, on banks and rocks, in dry, often calcareous soils across most of Europe, very locally in Britain and mainly in England and Wales.

Dark Mullein, *Verbascum nigrum*, has a clump of hairy, heart-shaped leaves, green on the upper surface, paler below. In summer its usually unbranched flowering spike reaches 2m (6ft) tall and bears many yellow or white flowers, purple-spotted at the base of each petal-lobe. As in all mulleins, the five stamens have hairy filaments, with purple hairs in this species. Plants grow on banks and in open places, often on roadsides, usually in dry, calcareous soils, in Great Britain and across most of Europe.

Great Mullein
Verbascum thapsus

White Mullein
Verbascum lychnitis

Dark Mullein
Verbascum nigrum

Figwort family

About 90 **Toadflaxes**, *Linaria* species, grow in Europe, the majority in the Mediterranean region. **Common Toadflax**, *L. vulgaris*, is found throughout Europe and much of the British Isles in grassy places, roadside verges, hedgebanks and waste places. It is a perennial plant with erect stems 30–90cm (1–3ft) tall, linear leaves and terminal spikes of bright yellow and orange flowers in summer. Each flower is two-lipped with a straight spur and an orange palate. This species has a long history of use in herbal medicine and was recommended for treating jaundice and dropsy. Steeped in milk it makes a good fly poison.

Pale Toadflax, *Linaria repens*, is one of several species with mauve or purple flowers. It forms erect stems about 30–90cm (1–3ft) tall with whorls of linear leaves and long terminal racemes of pale lilac or white flowers veined with darker violet and with an orange spot on the palate. Plants grow in dry, waste and cultivated places in western and central Europe, mainly in England and Wales in the British Isles.

Round-leaved Fluellen, *Kicksia spuria*, is an annual plant with sprawling, branched stems up to 50cm (20in) long and long-stalked, ovate or rounded leaves; stems and leaves are glandular and hairy. Solitary flowers appear on long stalks in the leaf axils in late summer; they are yellow with a violet upper lip and a long spur. Plants grow in arable fields, often in corn stubble, across most of Europe, locally in England and parts of Wales. Sharp-leaved Fluellen, *K. elatine*, is similar but has arrow-shaped leaves.

Common Toadflax
Linaria vulgaris

Pale Toadflax
Linaria repens

Round-leaved Fluellen
Kicksia spuria

Small Toadflax, *Chaenorhinum minus*, is a slender annual plant with branched, erect stems up to 25cm (10in) tall, linear leaves and small, solitary flowers in their axils. The flowers are purple with a yellow palate, an open mouth and a curved spur. This little plant grows in grassy places, arable land and waste ground, especially near railway lines, across much of Europe and the British Isles, except northern Scotland.

Small Toadflax
Chaenorhinum minus

Ivy-leaved Toadflax, *Cymbalaria muralis*, comes originally from Mediterranean Europe, but now grows wild further north and throughout most of the British Isles on old walls, sometimes on rocks. This is a small, hairless perennial with trailing, purplish stems rooting at the nodes and long-stalked, palmate, rather thick leaves. The little flowers grow on long stems in the leaf axils for much of the summer; they are blue-mauve with yellow palates and long spurs.

Ivy-leaved Toadflax
Cymbalaria muralis

Figworts are a group of some 300 *Scrophularia* species, about 40 of them found in Europe. They have erect, often square stems, opposite leaves and barrel-shaped flowers. Each flower has five small lobes around the mouth, often in two lips, with four fertile stamens and a single scale-like, sterile one inside.

Common Figwort, *S. nodosa*, is a perennial plant found in damp wasteland and hedgerows, in woods and beside streams throughout the British Isles and Europe. It has an erect stem up to 80cm (30in) tall, serrated, pointed-ovate leaves and many flowers in a branched inflorescence; the flowers are greenish with brown upper lips. At one time this plant was used in herb medicine; it was thought to be a cure for scrofula, a form of tuberculosis.

Common Figwort
Scrophularia nodosa

Figwort family

Monkeyflower
Mimulus guttatus

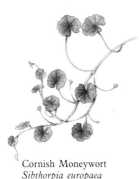

Mudwort
Limosella aquatica

Cornish Moneywort
Sibthorpia europaea

Monkeyflower, *Mimulus guttatus*, has been introduced into the British Isles and Europe from North America, becoming naturalized in wet places in many countries, on the banks of streams and ponds, and in marshes. It is a perennial, hairless plant, with leafy, creeping stems forming overlapping mats. In summer the shoots turn upwards and develop into erect stems 20–50cm (8–20in) tall with opposite, rounded leaves and showy yellow flowers in the axils of the upper leaves. The flowers are two-lipped, with orange spots on the palate.

Mudwort, *Limosella aquatica*, is found in wet mud around ponds, or in places subjected to periodic flooding; the plant is erratic in its appearance, coming and going with the water. It is an annual, with creeping stems rooting at the nodes and forming rosettes of linear, elliptical or spoon-shaped leaves, the stalks of the leaves several times longer than the blades. The white or pink flowers grow singly on separate stems and are bell-shaped with five petal-lobes. Mudwort is a relatively rare plant found mainly in England and Wales in the British Isles and across much of Europe.

Cornish Moneywort, *Sibthorpia europaea*, is another relatively rare plant, found locally in a few places in southern England and Wales, in southern Ireland and the Channel Islands, and in the mountains of western Europe and Greece. It grows in damp, shady places. This is a small perennial, with creeping, thread-like stems rooting at the nodes and many pale green leaves on long stalks. The leaf blades are rounded, often kidney-shaped, bluntly lobed into

5–7 sections at the margins. The flowers appear in late summer, growing singly on long stalks in the leaf axils; each one has five petal-lobes, the two upper lobes cream-coloured, the three lower pinkish.

Foxgloves, *Digitalis purpurea*, grow in acid soils in woods, heaths and mountains throughout the British Isles and in western and central Europe. This is a biennial plant, with a rosette of softly hairy, large, lance-shaped leaves in the first year and an erect, leafy flowering stem, 1–2m (3–6ft) tall, in the summer of the second. The flowers resemble large, tubular bells hanging in a one-sided spike; they are mauve-pink in colour, lighter on the inside with dark pink spots. Foxgloves are poisonous, containing the glycoside digitoxin which affects the heart. They are grown commercially for this drug which is used in medicine to regulate heart function.

Foxglove
Digitalis purpurea

Large Yellow Foxglove, *Digitalis grandiflora*, is a Continental species not found in the British Isles. It grows across much of Europe, except the north, in open, mountain woods, among rocks and on screes. This is a glandular-hairy, perennial plant, with an erect stem up to 1m (3ft) tall, with alternate, broadly lance-shaped leaves, shiny above, downy beneath. The stem ends in a long spike of hanging, pale yellow, tubular flowers, each one with a network of brown lines inside, hairy on the outside and with reflexed sepal-lobes. Small Yellow Foxglove, *D. lutea*, is similar, but its flowers are smaller, hairless on the outside and without the brown veins inside. It grows in woods and hills in central Europe. Both species are very poisonous.

Large Yellow Foxglove
Digitalis grandiflora

Figwort family

Speedwells, *Veronica* species, are mostly small, spreading plants with opposite leaves and blue or white flowers. Their flowers are distinctive, resembling a broad, upright cross with a short tube and four lobes. Two long stamens project beyond the petals towards the sides of the flower. About 300 *Veronica* species exist in temperate regions of the world, some 70 of them found in Europe.

Brooklime
*Veronica
beccabunga*

Water
Speedwell
Veronica anagallis-aquatica

Heath Speedwell
Veronica officinalis

Brooklime, *Veronica beccabunga*, is larger than most *Veronica* species, growing up to 60cm (2ft) tall. It is found in ponds and streams, in springs, marshes and wet meadows throughout Europe and the British Isles. This is a fleshy, perennial plant with sprawling stems which root in the mud and then turn upwards. It has opposite, rather thick, ovate leaves with serrated margins, and loose racemes of blue flowers in the upper leaf axils. Brooklime is edible and its young shoots can be eaten in salads like watercress.

Water Speedwell, *Veronica anagallis-aquatica*, is a similar but smaller plant, found also in ponds, streams and wet meadows throughout Europe and much of the British Isles. Its creeping, rooting stems grow 30cm (1ft) tall at most, its leaves are ovate on the lower stems, oblong with clasping bases higher up the stems, and its flowers are pale blue with darker veins.

Heath Speedwell, *Veronica officinalis*, is a typical small speedwell — a perennial plant with rooting stems often forming wide mats and other stems turning upwards to grow 40cm (15in) tall at most. It has softly hairy, oval or elliptical, toothed leaves and in summer dense, pyramidal racemes of lilac flowers appear, usually in one axil of a pair of leaves. This little plant grows in grassland, heaths and woods, usually in dry soils, throughout Europe and the British Isles.

Germander Speedwell, *Veronica chamaedrys*, has some of the bluest flowers in the plant world. This is another creeping, perennial plant with upturned stems; it has hairy, serrated leaves with short stalks, and flowers on long stalks in the upper leaf axils. The plant blooms in spring and early summer. It grows in woods and hedgerows, grassland, waste places and gardens throughout Europe and the British Isles. Thyme-leaved Speedwell, *V. serpyllifolia,* grows in similar places, has untoothed leaves and mauve-veined white flowers.

Germander Speedwell
Veronica chamaedrys

Wall Speedwell, *Veronica arvensis*, is a little annual plant with sprawling stems 25cm (10in) tall at most and coarsely toothed, ovate leaves; plants can be found in flower from spring to late autumn, with leafy spikes of tiny, bright blue flowers. They grow as weeds of cultivated land and gardens, in heaths and dry grassland, throughout Europe and the British Isles.

Wall Speedwell
Veronica arvensis

Ivy-leaved Speedwell, *Veronica hederifolia*, is another annual species, also a weed of cultivated land, found throughout Europe and much of the British Isles. It has hairy, branched, sprawling stems up to 60cm (2ft) long and forming mats with many kidney-shaped, palmately-lobed leaves, light green and rather thick for a speedwell. The pale blue flowers grow singly on long stalks in the upper leaf axils.

Ivy-leaved Speedwell
Veronica hederifolia

Figwort family

Many members of this family are semi-parasites with green stems and leaves, but poorly developed root systems. They attach themselves to the roots of other plants, especially to grasses, and obtain water and mineral salts from their hosts. All the following plants are semi-parasites.

Common Eyebright
Euphrasia rostkoviana

Eyebrights, *Euphrasia* species, are used in herb medicine to treat sore eyes. They are a complex group with about 50 species in Europe, many confined to specific habitats and with limited distributions. They are small annuals with branched, leafy stems and toothed, often opposite leaves. A spike-like inflorescence forms at the top of each stem, with solitary flowers in the axils of leaf-like bracts. The flowers are usually white or purple, two-lipped, with purple veins and a yellow blotch on the lower lip. **Common Eyebright**, *E. rostkoviana*, is taller than many, its branched stems up to 50cm (20in) tall. It grows in moist meadows in much of Europe, except the north, and throughout the British Isles.

Yellow Rattle
Rhinanthus minor

Yellow Rattle, *Rhinanthus minor*, is an annual plant with an erect, often branched, black-spotted stem up to 50cm (20in) tall and opposite, stalkless, toothed leaves. The two-lipped flowers are yellow, the upper lip of each flower hooded and the lower lip three-lobed. The flowers have characteristic inflated calyces, with reticulate veins and four teeth, becoming more inflated than ever in fruit, enclosing the flattened capsule with its winged seeds. The capsules dry out as they ripen, freeing the seeds so that they rattle inside when the wind blows. Yellow Rattle grows in grassy places, pastures, meadows and fens, often on basic or calcareous soils, throughout Europe and the British Isles.

Lousewort, *Pedicularis sylvatica*, is one of about 50 *Pedicularis* species found in Europe; they are poisonous plants, this one growing in marshes and bogs, damp heathland and moors across much of the Continent and the British Isles. It is a tufted perennial, with sprawling stems and deeply divided or pinnately lobed leaves, the leaflets toothed. The hooded, two-lipped, red or pink flowers appear in summer, borne in dense spikes with bracts like smaller leaves.

Lousewort
Pedicularis sylvatica

About 15 **Cow-wheats**, *Melampyrum* species, are found in Europe. They are poisonous, annual plants with simple, opposite leaves and tubular, two-lipped flowers; the upper lip is hooded and the lower lip three-lobed. **Common Cow-wheat**, *M. pratense*, grows locally in open woods and heaths throughout Europe and the British Isles. It is a small plant with branched, often sprawling, slender stems and ovate to linear leaves, flowering in summer. The yellow flowers grow singly in the axils of opposite, leaf-like bracts at the tops of the stems.

Common Cow-wheat
Melampyrum pratense

Red Bartsia, *Odontites verna*, grows in waste places, pastures, cultivated land and roadsides throughout Europe and the British Isles. It is a branched, annual plant with erect stems up to 50cm (20in) tall and opposite, lance-shaped leaves. The leaves have toothed margins and are often flushed with purple. In summer one-sided, leafy spikes of purplish-pink flowers appear at the tops of the stems; each flower has a hooded upper lip and a three-lobed lower lip.

Red Bartsia
Odontites verna

Figwort family

Toothwort, *Lathraea squamaria*, is a parasitic plant with rhizomes attached to tree roots, especially to those of hazel and elms, across much of Europe, Great Britain and eastern Ireland. In spring the white or pale pink flowering shoots appear, up to 30cm (1ft) tall (they lack chlorophyll), covered with fleshy, heart-shaped scale leaves and bearing flowers in a one-sided spike. Each purple-tinged, white flower grows in the axil of a bract, has a hairy calyx and a two-lipped corolla.

Toothwort
Lathraea squamaria

Common Broomrape
Orobanche minor

Broomrape family

Orobanchaceae About 10 genera and 170 species, mainly from warm temperate regions of the Old World. They are parasitic, often brownish herbs, lacking chlorophyll, their roots attached to those of other flowering plants and trees.

Family features Flowers hermaphrodite and bilaterally symmetrical; calyx toothed or lobed; corolla 5-lobed, often curved or 2-lipped; stamens 4 (2 long and 2 short) alternating with the corolla lobes; ovary superior with 1 cell. Fruit a capsule. These plants have erect stems, with alternate, often fleshy scale leaves at the base and dense, terminal spikes of flowers.

About 90 **Broomrapes**, *Orobanche* species, are found in Europe, parasitic on a variety of plants, some attacking crops like clovers or potatoes.
Common Broomrape, *O. minor*, has an erect, yellowish, purple-tinged stem up to 50cm (20in) tall, with brownish scale leaves and a loose spike of flowers, each one in the axil of a bract. The flowers are yellowish with purple veins.

The plant often grows on clovers and other members of the Pea family, also on Daisy family members, in meadows, on grassy roadsides and railway embankments, fixed dunes and cultivated land across Europe, mainly in the south in the British Isles.

Butterwort family

Lentibulariaceae A small family of insectivorous, often aquatic plants, with 4 genera and about 170 species found throughout the world.

   Family features Flowers hermaphrodite and bilaterally symmetrical. Calyx 5-lobed or 2-lipped; corolla 2-lipped and spurred; stamens 2; ovary superior with 1 cell. Fruit a capsule. Leaves form traps for insects.

The leaves of **Common Butterwort**, *Pinguicula vulgaris*, grow in a small rosette; their yellowish blades have a soft, slimy texture and rolled-up edges. Insects landing on the leaves are held and their struggles trigger the leaves into rolling up; the creatures are then digested. Purple flowers appear in early summer on erect, leafless stalks up to 15cm (6in) tall. Plants grow in bogs and wet heaths, or among wet rocks, across much of the British Isles and Europe.

Greater Bladderwort, *Utricularia vulgaris*, grows in lakes and ponds throughout Europe and the British Isles. It has many branching stems with dissected leaves floating beneath the surface. They bear traps — translucent bladders with hairs at one end which act as a trigger. If a water flea touches the hairs, a trap-door opens on the bladder and water rushes in, carrying the crustacean with it. In late summer yellow flowers appear above the water.

Common Butterwort
Pinguicula vulgaris

Greater Bladderwort
Utricularia vulgaris

Plantain family

Plantaginaceae About 3 genera and 270 species of herbaceous plants found mainly in northern temperate regions.

Plantains, a group of about 260 *Plantago* species, are annual or perennial plants, many with rosettes of basal leaves, unbranched flowering stalks and heads or spikes of small, dull flowers; each flower has four green sepals and four membranous petals. Their stamens are often conspicuous, with coloured anthers. The fruiting spikes remain long after flowering, finally breaking up into small, dry fruits.

Greater Plantain
Plantago major

Several plantains are weeds, like **Greater Plantain**, *Plantago major*, a perennial species found throughout the British Isles and Europe in lawns, on roadsides, waste and cultivated land, especially where the ground is well trodden. It has rosettes of broadly ovate, almost hairless leaves, their blades narrowing abruptly into stalks that are almost as long as the blades. In summer the narrow flowering spikes grow up to 60cm (2ft) tall, with green flowers and purple anthers.

Ribwort
Plantago lanceolata

Ribwort, *Plantago lanceolata*, has rosettes of more or less upright, lance-shaped leaves with a strongly ribbed appearance caused by their prominent, parallel veins. The flowering stalks grow up to 45cm (18in) tall in summer, ending in dense, cylindrical spikes of green flowers with whitish stamens. This common weed grows in grassy places, on roadsides and waste ground throughout Europe and the British Isles. Greater Plantain and Ribwort are both used as medicinal plants, making effective cough remedies.

Sea Plantain, *Plantago maritima*, forms several leaf rosettes growing from a woody base, with many thick, rather fleshy, linear leaves, sometimes toothed at the margins. The brownish flowers are borne in long, narrow spikes and have yellow anthers. This perennial plant grows in short grass near the sea, in salt marshes and beside mountain streams inland; it is found in most of Europe, around the British coasts and inland in the Scottish Highlands, the Welsh mountains, the Pennines and western Ireland.

Sea Plantain
Plantago maritima

Buck's-horn Plantain, *Plantago coronopus*, forms distinctive leaf rosettes, the leaves linear in shape and deeply toothed or pinnately lobed, their prostrate bases forming a circle on the ground and then turning upwards. The flowering stalks are also prostrate at the base, then turn upwards to bear long spikes of yellow-brown flowers with pale yellow anthers. Plants grow in dry, sandy or gravelly places or among rocks on the coasts of southern and central Europe, Britain and Ireland, inland in some areas of southern England.

Buck's-horn Plantain
Plantago coronopus

Shore-weed, *Littorella uniflora*, grows in acid water on the sandy shores of lakes and ponds or beside the sea. It is found across most of Europe, most commonly in Scotland and the Scottish islands in the British Isles, forming carpets of leaf rosettes submerged beneath the water surface and spreading over the mud. The leaves are linear and half-cylindrical, usually about 10cm (4in) long. The plants flower in the latter half of summer if they can grow above the surface; male and female flowers are separate, the male flowers borne singly at the top of a stalk with several female flowers at the base.

Shore-weed
Littorella uniflora

Dwarf Elder
Sambucus ebulus

Honeysuckle
Lonicera periclymenum

Lamb's Lettuce
Valerianella locusta

Honeysuckle family

Caprifoliaceae About 13 genera and 490 species of shrubs and herbs found in many parts of the world. Several shrubs are grown in gardens, including weigelas, honeysuckles and viburnums.

Family features Flowers usually in cymes, bilaterally symmetrical or regular, hermaphrodite. Calyx 5-toothed, often joined to ovary; corolla tubular, sometimes 2-lipped, formed of 4 or 5 fused petals; stamens 4 or 5, alternating with corolla-lobes; ovary inferior with 2–5 cells. Fruit is a berry, drupe or achene. Leaves opposite, simple or divided. Stipules 0 or small.

Dwarf Elder, *Sambucus ebulus*, grows in waste places, hedgerows and roadsides throughout Europe, scattered in the British Isles. It has a foetid scent and erect, grooved stems up to 120cm (4ft) tall, with pinnate leaves, each divided into 7–13 pointed-oblong leaflets with serrated margins. In the latter half of summer the plant bears flat-topped, umbel-like clusters of white flowers followed by black berries.

Honeysuckles, are a large group of about 260 *Lonicera* species, mostly shrubs and climbers. **Honeysuckle** or Woodbine, *L. periclymenum*, grows in woods and hedgerows in western and central Europe and is the only one native to the British Isles, where it is found throughout. It has twining, woody stems up to 6m (20ft) tall and dark green, pointed-ovate leaves. In summer the clusters of scented, creamy-yellow and pink flowers grow in leaf axils; they are tubular, with four petal-lobes at the top of the mouth and a single petal-lobe below. The flowers are followed by clusters of red berries.

Valerian family

Valerianaceae About 13 genera and 400 species of herbs found throughout the world, except in Australia.

Family features Flowers usually bilaterally symmetrical, hermaphrodite or unisexual; borne in dense, head-like inflorescences. Calyx usually toothed, often inrolled in flower and forming a feathery pappus in fruit; corolla often funnel-shaped, usually 5-lobed; stamens 1–3; ovary inferior with 1–3 cells. Fruit dry and indehiscent. Leaves opposite or in a rosette. Stipules 0.

Lamb's Lettuce or Corn Salad, *Valerianella locusta*, is a little, annual plant found on walls, in hedgebanks and dunes, in dry, arable and waste land throughout much of the British Isles and Europe. It has brittle, much-branched, leafy stems and head-like clusters of pale lilac flowers in summer.

About 25 **Valerians**, *Valeriana* species, grow in Europe. **Common Valerian**, *V. officinalis*, is a stout perennial with erect stems up to 1.5m (5ft) tall, large, pinnate leaves with lance-shaped, often toothed leaflets and clusters of pink or white flowers around midsummer. Plants grow in damp, grassy places and woods throughout Europe and the British Isles. Their roots are used in nerve tonics and sedatives.

Red Valerian, *Centranthus ruber*, is native to the Mediterranean region but has become naturalized in other parts of Europe, including southern areas of the British Isles, on cliffs and old walls. This perennial plant has stems up to 80cm (30in) tall, with grey-green, often toothed leaves and head-like clusters of showy red flowers around midsummer.

Common Valerian
Valeriana officinalis

Red Valerian
Centranthus ruber

Teasel family

Dipsacaceae About 9 genera and 155 species, mostly herbs, many from the Mediterranean region and western Asia.

Family features Flowers small, often borne in dense heads with an involucre; hermaphrodite or unisexual, bilaterally symmetrical. Calyx small, cup-like, deeply divided into sections or hairs; corolla has 4–5 lobes and is often 2-lipped; stamens 2 or 4, alternating with corolla lobes, their filaments free or joined in pairs; ovary inferior with 1 cell. Fruits dry and indehiscent. Leaves opposite or in whorls. Stipules 0.

Wild Teasel
Dipsacus fullonum

Wild Teasel, *Dipsacus fullonum*, grows in damp places, beside water, in woods and hedgerows, on roadsides, in field margins and by the sea throughout much of Europe and Great Britain. It is a biennial plant with a prickly flowering stem in the second year, often 1.5–2m (5–6ft) tall, and prickly leaves, lower ones joined across the stem to form cups. The pale purple flowers grow with prickly bracts in heads, opening in summer, forming a band which 'travels' up the head from bottom to top. 'Teasels' are the fruiting heads.

Field Scabious
Knautia arvensis

Field Scabious, *Knautia arvensis*, is a small, perennial plant found in dry, grassy places, roadsides, hedgebanks and woodland margins, especially on chalk or limestone, throughout Europe and much of the British Isles. It has rosettes of lance-shaped, somewhat toothed leaves in spring and erect, leafy flowering stems up to 1m (3ft) tall in late summer. The lilac-blue flowers are borne in flat heads, each with a ring of large flowers around the rim. The larger heads contain hermaphrodite flowers, smaller ones female flowers.

Small Scabious, *Scabiosa columbaria*, is also found in dry, calcareous grassland, on banks and pastures throughout Europe, England and Wales, north into southern Scotland. It is a perennial up to 60cm (2ft) tall, with stem leaves deeply divided into pinnate lobes. Its lilac-blue flowers are borne in heads with a ring of larger flowers around the circumference; all flowers are hermaphrodite. This is one of about 40 *Scabiosa* species found in Europe.

Devil's-bit Scabious, *Succisa pratensis*, grows in marshes and wet meadows throughout the British Isles and Europe. It is a perennial plant with a rosette of elliptical leaves and an erect stem up to 1m (3ft) tall in summer. This has a few narrow leaves and heads of mauve or blue-purple flowers; all the flowers are the same size. The heads may be small with female flowers, or larger with hermaphrodite flowers and protruding red-purple anthers.

Moschatel family

Adoxaceae The only member of this family is **Moschatel** or Townhall Clock, *Adoxa moschatellina*. It is a small perennial, 30cm (1ft) tall at most, with clumps of light green, more or less three-lobed leaves growing on long stems. In early summer it bears extraordinary yellow-green flowers in terminal clusters on stems that have a single leaf about halfway up. Each cluster has five flowers, four forming the sides of a square and the fifth on top facing the sky. The side flowers have three sepals and five petals, the top flower two sepals and four petals. Plants grow locally in woods and hedgerows across most of Europe and Great Britain.

Small Scabious
Scabiosa columbaria

Devil's-bit Scabious
Succisa pratensis

Moschatel
Adoxa moschatellina

Giant Bellflower
Campanula latifolia

Clustered
Bellflower
Campanula glomerata

Bellflower family

Campanulaceae About 60 genera and
2000 species, mostly herbs, found
throughout much of the world. The
family contains many garden plants,
including Canterbury Bells and lobelias.

Family features Flowers often
showy, regular or bilaterally
symmetrical, hermaphrodite. Calyx
usually 5-lobed and joined to the ovary;
corolla tubular, bell-shaped or 1- or
2-lipped; stamens as many as corolla-
lobes, alternating with the lobes; ovary
inferior, with 2 or more cells. Fruit a
capsule. Leaves alternate, simple.
Stipules 0. The plants usually contain
milky juice.

There are about 300 species of
Bellflowers, *Campanula* species, the
majority found in the Old World. Many
are perennial plants with erect, leafy
stems and blue, bell-like flowers in the
axils of the upper leaves. **Giant
Bellflower**, *C. latifolia*, is one such
species, found in woods and
hedgebanks, near streams and in
mountain meadows across most of
Europe and much of Great Britain. It
has clumps of pointed-ovate, basal
leaves and stout, erect stems, often 1m
(3ft) or more tall, leafy and with showy,
blue, bell-like flowers in the leaf axils,
each bell pointing upwards. This
species is often grown in gardens.

Clustered Bellflower, *Campanula
glomerata*, has its flowers clustered at
the top of the stems. It is a perennial
plant, its basal leaves long-stalked with
ovate blades, its flowering stems often
only 30cm (1ft) tall and leafy, with
stalkless leaves. It bears a terminal
cluster of stalkless, blue-purple bells
pointing upwards, and often has flowers

in the axils of the uppermost leaves as well. It grows in grassy places, often on chalk, also on cliffs and in open woods, mainly in southern and eastern England in Britain, and across most of Europe.

Harebell
Campanula rotundifolia

Harebell, *Campanula rotundifolia*, is a smaller perennial, its basal leaves long-stalked with rounded blades, its flowering stems slender and 40cm (15in) tall at most, with narrow leaves and nodding blue, bell-like flowers in the latter half of summer. Harebells grow in dry grassland, often on poor, shallow soils, on heaths and dunes throughout Europe and the British Isles. They are called Bluebells in Scotland.

Ivy-leaved Bellflower, *Wahlenbergia hederacea*, is a little, trailing, perennial plant with weak stems up to 30cm (1ft) long and palmately-lobed, long-stalked leaves. Pale blue, nodding, bell-like flowers appear in late summer. Plants grow in acid, peaty soils. on moors and heaths in western Europe, mainly in Wales and southwestern England in the British Isles.

Ivy-leaved Bellflower
Wahlenbergia hederacea

At first sight **Sheep's-bit**, *Jasione montana*, looks more like a scabious than a bellflower, for its blue flowers are borne in heads. This small, biennial plant has a rosette of narrow leaves in the first year and flowering stems up to 50cm (20in) tall in the second. These are leafy near the base with flower heads at the tops of long, bare stems in summer, each head cupped in two rows of leafy bracts and adorned with protruding purple anthers. Plants grow in sandy, often acid soils, in grassland, often on banks and cliffs, throughout Europe, mainly in the west in Great Britain, and around Ireland but not in the centre.

Sheep's-bit
Jasione montana

Daisy family

Compositae or Asteraceae. The largest family of flowering plants, with over 900 genera and 14,000 species found throughout the world. Most are herbs. The many decorative plants in the family include chrysanthemums, dahlias, gaillardias, asters, marigolds and many others. Food plants include lettuce, chicory and sunflowers. Some, like dandelions and thistles, are weeds.

Family features The flower structure in this family is unique. Individual flowers (called florets) are small but gathered into flower heads subtended by bracts; the heads look like single flowers. Each floret has a tubular or strap-shaped corolla; a flower head may be formed of all tubular florets or all strap-shaped florets, but often the tubular (or disk) florets form the centre of the head, with strap-shaped (or ray) florets around the margin. Each floret has a calyx formed of bristles, teeth or a membranous ring. Flowers may be male with 5 stamens, or female with an inferior ovary, or hermaphrodite. Fruits are hard achenes crowned by the pappus, the remains of the calyx.

Nodding Bur-marigold
Bidens cernua
.

Tripartite Bur-marigold
Bidens tripartita

Nodding Bur-marigold, *Bidens cernua*, is found beside streams and ponds throughout much of the British Isles and Europe. This annual plant has branched stems up to 60cm (2ft) tall, opposite, lance-shaped, toothed leaves and many nodding flower heads in late summer. The species has two varieties, one with yellow ray florets on the flower heads and one lacking ray florets. In both varieties there are leafy bracts behind the heads which are longer than the rays. As in all *Bidens* species, the fruits are barbed, the fruits of this species having four barbed spines.

Tripartite Bur-marigold, *Bidens tripartita*, also grows in ditches, beside streams and ponds locally throughout Europe and the British Isles, north to the south of Scotland and southern Scandinavia. It is similar to Bur-marigold but its leaves are cleft into three or five lance-shaped sections. The dull yellow flower heads have disk florets but no rays, and are cupped in green, leafy bracts.

Gallant Soldier, *Galinsoga parviflora*, came originally from South America but now grows in waste places and arable land in many parts of Europe and southern England. The plant grows up to 60cm (2ft) tall, has branched stems, ovate, toothed leaves and many little white flowers, each with five white ray florets and a yellow disk. It has many tiny fruits, flattened and bristly with parachutes of silvery scales.

Gallant Soldier
Galinsoga parviflora

Common Cocklebur, *Xanthium strumarium*, grows in waste places, beside rivers and roads in central and southern Europe; it has been introduced to the British Isles where it most often grows on rubbish tips in southeastern England. It is an annual plant with rough, branched stems and broad, rounded-triangular, often lobed leaves. Its male and female flowers are borne separately in rounded heads in the leaf axils, the female heads below the males. The female heads are prickly, enlarging in fruit to form ovoid burs with slender spines. The similar **Spiny Cocklebur**, *X. spinosum*, is an introduced plant from tropical America, found in waste land in many parts of Europe, including England and southern Scotland, usually near wool mills or ports. It is distinguished by its tripartite yellow spines and narrower, lobed leaves.

Common Cocklebur
Xanthium strumarium

Spiny Cocklebur
Xanthium spinosum

Goldenrod
*Solidago
virgaurea*

Sea Aster
Aster tripolium

Goldilocks
Aster linosyris

Daisy family

Goldenrods, about 120 *Solidago*
species, come mainly from North
America. Some are showy plants grown
in gardens for late summer colour but
the European **Goldenrod**, *S. virgaurea*,
is less impressive. This perennial plant
has a clump of lance-shaped, toothed
basal leaves and a leafy flowering stem
up to 75cm (30in) tall, with an
inflorescence of yellow flower heads on
straight, erect stems. Individual flower
heads are small, with the involucre
forming a cup for the yellow ray florets
and central yellow disk. Plants may be
found in dry woods and grassland, on
rocks and cliffs, hedgebanks and sand-
dunes throughout Europe and the
British Isles.

Michaelmas Daisies are a large group
of about 500 *Aster* species, many from
North America. Some are grown in
gardens, flowering in late summer or
autumn around Michaelmas. About 15
are native to Europe, such as **Sea
Aster**, *A. tripolium*, found in salt
marshes, on rocks and cliffs around
British and European coasts. It is a
perennial plant with branched stems up
to 1m (3ft) tall, narrow, fleshy leaves
and loose clusters of flower heads in late
summer; each head has bluish-purple
rays and a yellow disk.

Goldilocks, *Aster linosyris*, is a rather
different plant with rayless, yellow
flowers borne in dense, flat-topped
clusters at the tops of the stems in late
summer. It is a perennial, its erect
stems growing up to 50cm (20in) tall,
and clothed with numerous linear
leaves. It grows in rocky places, on cliffs
and open grassland, usually on
calcareous soils, across much of Europe,

but its numbers are declining and it is rare in Britain, found only on limestone cliffs in a few places on the coasts of southwest England and Wales.

The **Fleabanes**, members of the genus *Erigeron*, are another large group of over 200 species, sometimes mistaken for asters but flowering in early rather than late summer. **Blue Fleabane**, *E. acer*, is a roughly hairy, annual or biennial plant, with a clump of oblong basal leaves and an erect, leafy stem up to 40cm (15in) tall, branching to bear a cluster of small flower heads. The leaves are narrow with half-clasping bases; the flower heads have erect blue-purple ray florets not much longer than the yellow disk is wide. Plants grow in dry grassland, on banks and walls, especially on calcareous soils, across Europe and in England and Wales, locally in Ireland.

Blue Fleabane
Erigeron acer

Canadian Fleabane, *Conyza canadensis*, has been introduced into many parts of Europe, England and Wales from North America, now growing in waste and cultivated land. This is a coarse, bristly, annual plant with a rosette of basal leaves and a stem up to 1m (3ft) tall, very leafy with lance-shaped, more or less toothed leaves. From the upper leaf axils grow clusters of tiny flowers, each with minute white rays and a yellow disk.

Canadian
Fleabane
Conyza canadensis

Daisies, *Bellis perennis*, grow in lawns and other places with short grass throughout the British Isles and Europe. They form small rosettes of spoon-shaped leaves and flower for much of the year, producing many solitary flower heads on leafless stalks. The ray florets may be white or tinged with pink.

Daisy
Bellis perennis

Daisy family

Stinking Chamomile, *Anthemis cotula*, grows in waste places and arable land, generally on heavy soils, throughout Europe, mainly in England and Wales in the British Isles. It has an unpleasant odour and can cause blisters if handled. This annual plant has a branched stem up to 60cm (2ft) tall, soft, dissected leaves and daisy-like flowers in summer; these have white ray florets and dome-shaped, yellow disks. The true Chamomile, *Chamaemelum nobile*, used in chamomile tea and grown in chamomile lawns, grows wild in western Europe, southern England, Wales and Ireland, in grassy places, on heaths and commons, banks and roadsides. It forms a mat of creeping stems and pleasantly scented, feathery leaves, with daisy-like flower heads in summer.

Scentless Mayweed, *Tripleurospermum inodorum*, is an annual, almost scentless plant with a branched, sprawling stem up to 60cm (2ft) tall and leaves divided into linear segments. In the latter part of summer it bears daisy-like flowers, each with a domed yellow disk and white ray florets which droop as they age. This is an abundant weed of cultivated and waste land throughout the British Isles and Europe. The sprawling stems and fleshy leaves of the related Sea Mayweed, *T. maritimum*, grow on the drift lines of shingle beaches, on cliffs and rocks, on the sea-edge of sand-dunes all around the British Isles and on the coasts of western and northern Europe.

Wild Chamomile or Scented Mayweed, *Matricaria recutita*, is an aromatic annual plant with divided, fern-like leaves and many daisy-like

Stinking Chamomile
Anthemis cotula

Scentless Mayweed
Tripleurospermum inodorum

Wild
Chamomile
Matricaria recutita

flower heads around midsummer. The flowers have domed yellow disks and white rays which become reflexed soon after the flowers open. This is a common weed of arable and waste land, found across much of Europe, in England and Wales, rarely in Scotland or Ireland. Tea made from its flowers is useful for treating digestive disorders.

Pineapple Weed
Matricaria matricarioides

Pineapple Weed, *Matricaria matricarioides*, is an introduced weed found in waste places and roadsides throughout the British Isles and Europe. It is an annual plant with a branched, often sprawling stem about 30cm (1ft) tall and pinnate leaves divided into linear segments, smelling of pineapples if crushed. Its flower heads are distinctive, each with a highly domed, greenish-yellow disk cupped in green bracts; they have no ray florets.

Corn Marigold
Chrysanthemum segetum

Corn Marigold, *Chrysanthemum segetum*, was once a cornfield weed but is now most often found in waste places and on roadsides, growing locally in the British Isles and across Europe. It is a greyish annual plant with erect, branched stems up to 60cm (2ft) tall and irregularly toothed, oblong leaves, their bases clasping the stems. The all-yellow flowers appear in summer.

Ox-eye Daisy, *Leucanthemum vulgare*, is a common grassland plant found throughout the British Isles and Europe. But it is also grown in gardens, usually as large-flowered varieties known as Marguerites, Moon Daisies and Shasta Daisies. It forms spreading clumps of leaf rosettes and erect stems up to 1m (3ft) tall, each with dark green, pinnately divided leaves and a single large, daisy-like flower with white ray florets and a flat yellow disk.

Ox-eye Daisy
Leucanthemum vulgare

Daisy family

Yarrow
Achillea millefolium

Sneezewort
Achillea ptarmica

Tansy
Tanacetum vulgare

Yarrow or Milfoil, *Achillea millefolium*, is an aromatic plant used in herb medicine as a remedy for colds. It grows in meadows, grassy banks, roadsides and hedgerows throughout Europe and the British Isles, forming spreading colonies with ferny, much-dissected, dark green leaves and erect flowering stems with more or less flattened, terminal clusters of white flower heads. Each head is small, with about five broad ray florets around each disk.

Sneezewort, *Achillea ptarmica*, is a taller plant, with erect stems up to 60cm (2ft) tall, lance-shaped leaves with serrated margins, and branched, terminal clusters of larger white flower heads. It grows in marshes, damp meadows and beside streams throughout the British Isles and much of Europe.

Tansy, *Tanacetum vulgare*, is an old medicinal plant, at one time strewn over corpses to keep worms and flies away, now occasionally used to bathe sprains and bruises. It is a perennial, with erect robust stems and soft, ferny, pinnately divided leaves. In the latter half of summer, when the stems are about 1m (3ft) tall, they bear terminal, branched clusters of yellowish flower heads; the heads contain only disk florets, many of them packed together.

Feverfew, *Tanacetum parthenium*, is another medicinal herb, traditionally used to reduce fevers but also effective as an insecticide like pyrethrum. This perennial plant has a branched, erect stem about 60cm (2ft) tall, pinnately divided leaves and small, daisy-like flower heads in the latter part of summer. It is native to southeastern

Europe but is also introduced further north and in Great Britain, found most often on walls, on roadsides and in waste places, but also grown in gardens.

The **Wormwoods**, some 400 members of the genus *Artemisia*, are generally aromatic, herbaceous or shrubby plants, about 50 of which grow in Europe. Some, like Wormwood and Tarragon, are culinary and medicinal herbs; others, like Southernwood, are grown in gardens for their silver or grey foliage.

Wormwood, *Artemisia absinthium*, is best known for giving the bitter taste to absinthe but is also a medicinal herb. It is a perennial, silky-hairy plant with rosettes of thrice-pinnate leaves and erect, leafy flowering stems, often woody at the base, up to 1m (3ft) tall in summer. The stems are grooved and angled, branching to form inflorescences of small, yellowish flower heads. The heads are rounded and drooping, and contain only disk florets. Plants grow in rocky and uncultivated places across Europe, in waste places and on roadsides in England and Wales, rarely in Scotland and Ireland.

Mugwort, *Artemisia vulgaris*, is a perennial weed found in waste places and roadsides throughout Europe and the British Isles. It has erect, reddish stems up to 120cm (4ft) tall, with clasping, deeply cleft leaves, dark green above, white with cottony hairs below. In late summer the plant produces numerous small, reddish-brown flower heads growing on long, branched, leafy stems from every leaf axil. It is strongly aromatic and used in herb medicine to treat digestive disorders; in Europe it is added to stuffings and sauces for eating with geese.

Feverfew
Tanacetum parthenium

Wormwood
Artemisia absinthium

Mugwort
Artemisia vulgaris

Daisy family

Coltsfoot, *Tussilago farfara*, flowers in early spring before its leaves emerge. The flower heads are yellow, formed of ray florets and borne singly on reddish, scaly stems only 15cm (6in) tall, often appearing in large clumps. The flowers are followed by clock-like fruits and finally the white-felted leaves emerge. They grow large and rounded, shallowly lobed and deep green above once mature. This plant grows in arable land, on banks and in waste places, on cliffs and landslides, shingle banks and dunes, riversides and woodland margins, often in damp places. It is rich in mucilage and an effective cough remedy.

Like Coltsfoot, **Butterbur**, *Petasites hybridus*, blooms before the leaves emerge. It forms patches of thick, purplish flowering shoots in spring, with greenish scale-leaves and pale red-violet flower heads. Plants bear either male or female flowers, the male heads mostly formed of tubular florets, the female flowers of strap-shaped florets. In female plants the flowering stems grow about twice as tall after flowering and develop hairy fruits. The large leaves emerge in summer, grey-downy at first and growing up to 90cm (3ft) across, shaped like rounded hearts with toothed margins and hollow, channelled stalks. Butterbur grows beside streams, in wet meadows, marshes and woods across Europe and the British Isles. Most British plants are male.

Groundsels and **Ragworts** belong to the large genus *Senecio*, with about 100 species worldwide, including herbs, shrubs and climbers. Some 65 species are found in Europe. **Common Ragwort**, *S. jacobaea*, is a biennial or

Coltsfoot
Tussilago farfara

Butterbur
Petasites hybridus

Common
Ragwort
Senecio jacobaea

perennial plant with sinuate basal leaves and erect, leafy flowering stems up to 1.5m (5ft) tall. The stems are furrowed, often cottony, with crisped, sinuate leaves, dark green above and paler beneath. The stems branch to bear flat-topped inflorescences of golden yellow flower heads with green, black-tipped bracts followed by fruits with hairy parachutes. This plant is poisonous to grazing animals, retaining its poisons in hay or silage and causing many livestock deaths each year. It is abundant in overgrazed pastures, waste places and roadsides, on sand-dunes and open woods throughout Europe and the British Isles.

Oxford Ragwort, *Senecio squalidus*, is an annual plant with sprawling stems only 30cm (1ft) tall, dark green, pinnately lobed leaves and an irregular inflorescence of golden yellow flower heads, each head borne in a bell-shaped cup of black-tipped bracts. The species comes from the mountains of central and southern Europe but has been introduced into western Europe and the British Isles. It grows in waste places, on roadsides and railway embankments, in arable land and on walls throughout lowland areas of England, locally in southern Scotland and southern Ireland.

Oxford Ragwort
Senecio squalidus

Groundsel, *Senecio vulgaris*, is an annual weed found in fields, gardens, waste places and roadsides worldwide. It has a branched stem no more than 30cm (1ft) tall, with crisp, irregularly toothed leaves and many small flower heads. Each head has a cup of green, black-tipped bracts and many yellow disk florets so that it resembles a shaving brush. The flowers do not have ray florets. After flowering, each head becomes a dome of white-haired fruits.

Groundsel
Senecio vulgaris

Daisy family

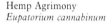

Hemp Agrimony, *Eupatorium cannabinum*, is the only species of this large genus found in Europe; most of the 1200 members are American. It is a large perennial plant with a clump of erect, often reddish, leafy stems up to 120cm (4ft) tall, with opposite, palmately-lobed leaves. The leaves have lance-shaped, serrated leaflets. The stems branch at the top to form dense, flat-topped inflorescences of fluffy, reddish-mauve flowers; the flowers are all tubular, their fluffy appearance coming from the protruding white styles. This plant grows in damp and wet places, in marshes and fens, on the banks of rivers and in wet woods throughout Europe and most of the British Isles.

Hemp Agrimony
Eupatorium cannabinum

Elecampane
Inula helenium

Elecampane, *Inula helenium*, is an ancient herbal plant used to treat asthma and chest complaints. It grows in waste places and hedgerows, woods and rough pastures, scattered across Europe, Great Britain and Ireland, probably naturalized in most of this area and only native to southeastern Europe. It is a stout, softly hairy perennial, with a rosette of pointed-ovate leaves, each up to 60cm (2ft) long, and thick stems up to 1.5m (5ft) tall, bearing similar but smaller leaves, their bases clasping the stem. The stems branch near the top to bear clusters of bright yellow flower heads, with hemispherical involucres and numerous long, narrow ray florets around yellow disks.

Irish Fleabane, *Inula salicina*, is a much more slender perennial, with stiff, leafy stems up to 50cm (20in) tall, the lower leaves lance-shaped and upper ones pointed heart-shaped with clasping

Irish Fleabane
Inula salicina

bases. The flower heads terminate the stems and smaller ones may grow on side shoots in the upper leaf axils; each head has a hemispherical involucre of bracts, numerous yellow ray florets and a central yellow disk. This plant grows in rocky and wooded slopes, in wet calcareous grassland and marshes throughout Europe, but in the British Isles is confined to the limestone shores of Lough Derg in Ireland.

Ploughman's Spikenard, *Inula conyza*, is a biennial or perennial plant. It has a rosette of ovate, softly hairy basal leaves and erect, purplish stems up to 120cm (4ft) tall, with downy, pointed-elliptical leaves and a branched, terminal cluster of flower heads in late summer. Each head is cupped in an involucre, the outer bracts green and the inner ones purplish; the florets are yellowish, the inner ones tubular and the outer ones often with small rays. Plants grow in dry, calcareous soils, in open woods and grassy places, on rocky slopes and cliffs throughout much of Europe, except the north, in England and Wales north to Cumbria.

Ploughman's Spikenard
Inula conyza

Golden Samphire, *Inula crithmoides*, is a maritime plant growing on cliffs and rocks, on shingle banks and salt marshes, locally on the coasts of western Europe south to the Mediterranean, around the coasts of England, Wales and southern Ireland. This perennial, rather shrubby species has branched, fleshy stems about 60cm (2ft) tall and many linear or lance-shaped leaves which often have three teeth at their tips. The plants flower in the latter half of summer, with a branched inflorescence of many flower heads; they have golden yellow ray florets and orange-yellow disks.

Golden Samphire
Inula crithmoides

Daisy family

Fleabane, *Pulicaria dysenterica*, is a perennial plant, hoary with white hairs. It has erect, leafy stems up to 60cm (2ft) tall and oblong to lance-shaped leaves with wavy margins, the higher ones with heart-shaped, clasping bases. The stems branch near the top to form clusters of yellow flower heads, each with a yellow disk and linear ray florets. The flowers are followed by hairy fruits. Plants grow in wet meadows and marshes, beside streams and ditches throughout much of Europe, except the north, in England and into southern Scotland, in Wales and Ireland. At one time they were burned to deter fleas.

Everlasting Flowers, are members of several genera with dry, papery flowers which last far longer than most blooms. Some, like the helichrysums, are used in dried flower arrangements. **Mountain Everlasting**, *Antennaria dioica*, is a small perennial plant with creeping stems and mats of leaf rosettes, the spoon-shaped leaves green on the upper surface, white woolly beneath. Its flowering stems grow 20cm (8in) tall and bear terminal clusters of small flower heads in summer, males and females on separate plants. The smaller male heads have white bracts, like ray florets, around the tubular florets; female heads have pink bracts held erect. Plants grow in dry mountain meadows and heaths, on slopes and banks, usually on calcareous or base-rich soils, in northern and central Europe, mainly in Scotland and the Scottish islands, northern England and Ireland in the British Isles.

Cudweeds are woolly-haired members of two genera, *Filago* and *Gnaphalium*.

Fleabane
Pulicaria dysenterica

Mountain Everlasting
Antennaria dioica

About 12 *Filago* and seven *Gnaphalium* species are found in Europe. **Common Cudweed**, *F. vulgaris*, has erect, often branched stems about 30cm (1ft) tall, with white-woolly, linear, often wavy leaves and clusters of tiny flower heads at the tips of all the branches. The heads contain yellow tubular florets, the outer ones female and inner ones hermaphrodite; they are cupped in woolly outer bracts and membranous, yellowish inner bracts, all half sunk into white woolly hairs. Plants grow in acid, sandy soils, in dry grassland and heaths, fields and roadsides throughout Europe and Great Britain north to southern Scotland, occasionally in Ireland.

Heath Cudweed, *Gnaphalium sylvaticum*, grows in dry heaths and open woods, grassland and commons, on acid soils throughout Europe and the British Isles. It is a perennial plant with sprawling, leafy non-flowering shoots and erect flowering shoots up to 60cm (2ft) tall. These bear dense clusters of flower heads in the leaf axils; the heads are pale brown, formed of disk florets and cupped in bracts. The outer bracts are brown with clear tips, the inner bracts with a green stripe in the centre and pink or white tips and margins.

Marsh Cudweed, *Gnaphalium uliginosum*, is found on the banks of streams and ditches, in woodland rides, damp arable fields and gardens, generally on acid soils, throughout Europe and the British Isles. This inconspicuous plant is no more than 20cm (8in) tall, an annual with grey, woolly stems and leaves. The stem is branched with linear leaves and bears small clusters of little, brownish-white flower heads in the leaf axils and terminating the stems in late summer.

Common Cudweed
Filago vulgaris

Heath Cudweed
Gnaphalium sylvaticum

Marsh Cudweed
Gnaphalium uliginosum

Daisy family

Most common **Thistles** belong to two genera, *Carduus* and *Cirsium*. There are about 120 *Carduus* species altogether, with about 45 in Europe, and about 150 *Cirsium* species, with 65 or so in Europe. Thistles are more or less spiny plants, with alternate, toothed, often prickly leaves and flower heads formed only of disk florets cupped in involucres of overlapping, spiny bracts. Most have red or purple flowers. One of the best ways to distinguish between the two genera is to look at the achenes. In *Carduus* species the hairs on the achenes are simple and unbranched, while in *Cirsium* species the hairs are feathery.

Creeping Thistle
Cirsium arvense

Spear Thistle
Cirsium vulgare

Creeping Thistle, *Cirsium arvense*, is an aggressive weed found in arable and waste land, roadsides, open woods and pastures throughout the British Isles and Europe. It forms patches of erect, unwinged stems up to 1.5m (5ft) tall, with wavy, lobed, spiny-edged leaves. The pale purple flower heads are solitary or borne in small clusters in the upper leaf axils, male and female heads usually on separate plants. Although many brown-haired fruits are formed, few contain viable seed. Only when male and female plants grow together are fertile seeds produced.

Spear Thistle, *Cirsium vulgare*, is a weed of gardens, roadsides and waste places, especially in calcareous or base-rich soils, throughout the British Isles and Europe. It is a biennial plant with a rosette of deeply divided, spine-tipped, wavy leaves in the first year and a flowering stem up to 1.5m (5ft) tall in the second. The stem is furrowed and cottony with spiny, interrupted wings and large, deeply lobed, spiny leaves.

The flower heads are borne on long stalks in the upper leaf axils, singly or in small clusters; they are large and showy, with spiny involucres and red-purple florets, and followed by white-haired fruits.

Marsh Thistle, *Cirsium palustre*, resembles Creeping Thistle to some extent, but is a biennial and lacks creeping roots; its stems are interruptedly spiny-winged, its many flower heads are dark red-purple and its fruits have dirty white hairs. Plants grow in damp places, in wet meadows and marshes, in woods and hedgerows throughout Europe and the British Isles.

Marsh Thistle
Cirsium palustre

Stemless Thistles, *Cirsium acaule*, grow in short grassland on the downs and limestone uplands of southern England and across Europe, forming flat rosettes of spiny, lobed leaves. In late summer the flowers appear — a single bright red-purple flowering head at the centre of each rosette. This plant is no longer as common as it once was, since so many of the downs are now wheat fields.

Stemless Thistle
Cirsium acaule

Melancholy Thistle, *Cirsium helenioides*, forms a patch of erect, cottony, very leafy stems up to 120cm (4ft) tall. But its leaves are not typical thistle ones, being broadly lance-shaped, thin and flaccid, white-felted beneath with softly prickly margins, the upper ones with clasping bases. There is a solitary flower head at the top of each stem, the florets red-purple, the involucre broadly egg-shaped with purple-tipped bracts. Plants grow in hills and mountains, beside streams, in damp meadows and open woods across much of Europe, in northern England, Scotland and north Wales.

Melancholy
Thistle
*Cirsium
helenioides*

Daisy family

Musk Thistle
Carduus nutans

Musk Thistle, *Carduus nutans*, is a biennial with a rosette of wavy, spiny leaves in the first year and a cottony, narrowly spine-winged flowering stem up to 1m (3ft) tall in the second. This bears deeply lobed leaves with wavy, spiny margins and large, drooping flower heads, solitary or borne in small clusters, formed of purple disk florets and surrounded by large, reflexed, spine-tipped bracts. Plants grow in waste places and roadsides, fields and pastures across much of Europe, in England, Wales and southern Scotland.

Welted Thistle
Carduus acanthoides

Welted Thistle, *Carduus acanthoides*, is another biennial, with a rosette of wavy-lobed, spiny leaves in the first year and a branched flowering stem up to 120cm (4ft) tall in the second. The stems have continuous narrow, spiny wings and lobed, wavy leaves with weak spines on their margins. The reddish-purple flower heads are borne in dense clusters and held erect over involucres of linear, spine-tipped bracts. Plants grow in damp, grassy places, beside rivers, on roadsides and in hedgerows in many lowland areas of the British Isles and across much of Europe.

Slender Thistle, *Carduus tenuiflorus*, may be annual or biennial, has a branched stem up to 120cm (4ft) tall, continuous spiny wings and wavy-lobed, spiny-margined leaves, their bases running into the wings. Its flowers are small, with pale purple-red florets over cylindrical involucres; they are borne in dense, terminal clusters. This plant grows in dry, grassy and waste places, and on roadsides, especially near the sea, in western Europe and much of the British Isles, except the north.

Slender Thistle
Carduus tenuiflorus

Scotch Thistle or Cotton Thistle, *Onopordon acanthium*, is a large biennial plant with erect, broadly spine-winged, white-cottony stems up to 1.5m (5ft) tall. It has large, prickly-margined leaves and solitary purple flower heads terminating its many branches. The heads are cupped in rounded involucres of spiny bracts. Plants grow in fields, waste places, roadsides and hedgebanks throughout Europe and have been introduced to England and Wales, more rarely to Scotland.

Scotch Thistle
Onopordon acanthium

Milk Thistle, *Silybum marianum*, comes from southern Europe but is also naturalized along roadsides, in cultivated and waste land through central Europe, and in many lowland areas of Great Britain. This is an annual or biennial plant, with a rosette of lobed, pale green, white-mottled leaves with spiny margins. The erect stem grows up to 120cm (4ft) tall, has clasping leaves and in early summer produces solitary, nodding flower heads with red-purple florets.

Milk Thistle
Silybum marianum

Carline Thistle, *Carlina vulgaris*, is a biennial plant with a rosette of cottony leaves in the first year and an erect flowering stem up to 60cm (2ft) tall in the second. The stem leaves are numerous, wavy with weak spines on their lobed margins and half-clasping bases. Flower heads appear in late summer; each is formed of golden disk florets encircled by an outer ring of spiny, greenish bracts and an inner ring of conspicuous, pointed, shiny-yellow ones. The yellow bracts spread out in dry weather and close up in wet. Plants grow in dry, usually calcareous grassland throughout Europe, in England, Wales and central Ireland, on the east coast of Scotland and the Inner Hebrides.

Carline Thistle
Carlina vulgaris

Daisy family

Burdocks grow in waste places and on roadsides, in fields and open woods, **Lesser Burdock**, *Arctium minus*, commonly throughout Europe and the British Isles, **Greater Burdock**, *A. lappa*, scattered across much of Europe and in lowland areas of England and Wales. Lesser Burdock grows about 120cm (4ft) tall, Greater Burdock about 1.5m (5ft). Both are bushy plants with furrowed, reddish stems and large, long-stalked, pointed-ovate and rather heart-shaped leaves, those of Lesser Burdock rather narrower. Their flower heads have red-purple tubular florets and an involucre of hooked bracts. In Lesser Burdock the heads are usually less than 2.5cm (1in) across and borne in tight clusters in the leaf axils; in Greater Burdock the heads grow 3–4cm (1¼ – 1¾in) across and are borne on long stalks. The fruits are hooked 'burs', those of Greater Burdock straw-coloured and often open, those of Lesser Burdock darker and closed at the top.

Saw-wort, *Serratula tinctoria*, grows in damp grassland and marshes, woodland rides and margins, often in calcareous soils, scattered throughout Europe and Great Britain. This is a perennial plant with wiry, erect stems, its leaves varying from undivided to pinnately lobed with bristle-tipped teeth on the margins. In late summer it produces terminal clusters of reddish-purple flower heads in involucres formed of chaffy scales. The fruits are hairy with many rows of bristly rough, hairs.

The genus *Centaurea* is a large one, with about 200 species in Europe. **Greater Knapweed**, *C. scabiosa*, is a striking perennial plant that usually

Lesser Burdock
Arctium minus

Greater Burdock
Arctium lappa

Saw-wort
Serratula tinctoria

grows in calcareous soils in dry grassland and hedgebanks, among rocks and on cliffs throughout Europe and much of the British Isles, rarely in Scotland. It has erect, grooved stems up to 90cm (3ft) tall, with dark green, pinnately divided leaves, the stems branching to bear flower heads in the latter half of summer. The heads are conspicuous, reddish-purple and formed of tubular florets with the large outer florets much divided. The bracts of the involucre are fringed with what look like blackish, horseshoe-shaped combs. At one time this plant was used in herb medicine to treat wounds and bruises.

Greater
Knapweed
Centaurea scabiosa

Lesser Knapweed or Hardheads, *Centaurea nigra*, grows in dry grassland, on cliffs and among rocks, on roadsides and railway embankments throughout western Europe and the British Isles. It is another summer-flowering perennial, with tough, erect stems up to 60cm (2ft) tall, sinuate basal leaves and entire stem leaves, and red-purple flower heads, usually with the marginal florets the same as all the others. The bracts of the involucre have triangular tips with brown or black fringes.

Lesser Knapweed
Centaurea nigra

Cornflower or Bluebottle, *Centaurea cyanus*, was once an agricultural weed but is now more likely to be found on roadsides and waste places throughout Europe and Great Britain. It is not common in the wild but is grown in gardens. This is an annual plant with a wiry, grooved, branched stem up to 90cm (3ft) tall, linear leaves and numerous, usually blue flower heads with tubular florets; the marginal florets are large and conspicuous. The involucre of each flower head is bell-shaped and the bracts have fringed, membranous edges.

Cornflower
Centaurea cyanus

Daisy family

Chicory, *Cichorium intybus*, grows in rough pastures, roadsides, fields and waste places throughout Europe and the British Isles, most commonly in lowland areas and on calcareous soils. It is also cultivated for its young shoots, which are eaten as a vegetable and in salads. The tap roots are roasted, ground and added to coffee. Chicory is a perennial plant with a branched stem up to 120cm (4ft) tall, wavy-toothed leaves and bright blue flower heads composed of strap-shaped florets. They grow in clusters in the upper leaf axils.

Chicory
Cichorium intybus

Nipplewort, *Lapsana communis*, is an annual plant with erect, leafy stems up to 120cm (4ft) tall, branching into a complex inflorescence. The lower leaves are thin, each with a large terminal lobe and several small lobes or a wing near the base; upper leaves are lance-shaped. The many flower heads are small, formed of lemon-yellow ray florets, and appear for much of the summer. This is a weed of roadsides and waste places, woodland margins and hedgerows, walls, gardens and cultivated land throughout Europe and the British Isles. Its young leaves can be eaten raw in salads or cooked like spinach.

Nipplewort
Lapsana communis

Cat's-ear, *Hypochoeris radicata*, is like a hairy dandelion with tough, solid flowering stems which fork to bear several flower heads in early summer. The heads are formed of yellow ray florets, the outer rays greenish-grey beneath and cupped in involucres of small, bristly bracts. Plants are common on grassy roadside verges, in meadows and pastures, on commons and stabilized sand-dunes, sometimes in gardens, throughout Europe and the British Isles.

Cat's-ear
Hypochoeris radicata

Autumnal Hawkbit, *Leontodon autumnalis*, is a perennial with a rosette of pinnately lobed leaves with deep, narrow lobes, and several solid stems, forking to bear yellow flower heads. The heads are streaked with red on the undersides and cupped in an involucre of overlapping bracts. This is a common weed of grassy places, meadows, pastures and roadsides throughout Europe and the British Isles.

Autumnal
Hawkbit
Leontodon autumnalis

Bristly Ox-tongue, *Picris echioides*, is an annual or biennial plant found on roadsides and hedgebanks, in fields and waste places, particularly on calcareous clay soils; it is probably native to the Mediterranean region but is naturalized in central Europe, lowland areas of England and Wales, southern and central Ireland. It has stout, branched stems up to 90cm (3ft) tall with lance-shaped, wavy-margined leaves, all covered in bristly hairs with swollen, whitish bases. It blooms in summer and into autumn, with dense clusters of flower heads formed of yellow ray florets. Each head is cupped in large, bristly, heart-shaped bracts. The fruits have white, feathery hairs.

Bristly
Ox-tongue
Picris echioides

Hawkweed Ox-tongue, *Picris hieracioides*, also has bristly hairs, but they lack swollen bases. This is a biennial or perennial plant, with branched, spreading stems up to 90cm (3ft) tall and rough, wavy-margined, lance-shaped leaves. The flowers have yellow ray florets but their involucres have normal-size, spreading bracts. The fruits have feathery, cream-coloured hairs. Plants grow in grassy places, on roadsides and walls, on rocky slopes and in vineyards, especially on calcareous soils, throughout Europe, in lowland areas of England and Wales.

Hawkweed
Ox-tongue
Picris hieracioides

Daisy family

Goatsbeard
Tragopogon pratensis

Goatsbeard or Jack-go-to-bed-at-noon, *Tragopogon pratensis*, may be an annual or perennial plant with a rosette of long, linear, white-veined leaves. The flowering stem is little branched, about 60cm (2ft) tall, with longer leaves and large, terminal flower heads which close in the afternoon. They are formed of yellow ray florets, the slender bracts beneath the heads projecting beyond the florets. The fruiting heads are formed from large balls of achenes, each with a feathery parachute, the hairs from one achene interwoven with those adjacent. Plants grow in meadows and pastures, roadsides and waste places, sometimes on fixed sand-dunes, throughout much of Europe, in lowland areas of Great Britain and in central Ireland.

About 16 Lettuces, *Lactuca* species, are found in Europe. **Prickly Lettuce**, *L. serriola*, grows in waste places and on walls, sometimes on fixed sand-dunes, across much of Europe, in southern England and Wales. It is an annual plant with a rosette of more or less oblong leaves, often with wavy margins, prickly on the edges and on the veins beneath. The stems grow up to 2m (6ft) tall and are very leafy, the upper leaves with clasping bases; when the plants grow in full sun, the leaves are held vertically in the north/south plane. By late summer the stems end in branched inflorescences of small, pale yellow flower heads, together with clusters of parachuted seeds. Garden Lettuces are varieties of *L. sativa*.

Wall Lettuce, *Mycelis muralis*, is a related perennial plant, with an erect stem up to 1m (3ft) tall, pinnately lobed leaves — the lower ones with winged

Prickly Lettuce
Lactuca serriola

Wall Lettuce
Mycelis muralis

stalks, the upper ones simpler, often reddish, with clasping bases — and large, spreading inflorescences of small yellow flowers cupped in cylindrical involucres. Each head contains only five ray florets. Plants grow among rocks, in hedgebanks and waste places, cultivated land and open woods, often on base-rich or calcareous soils, throughout Europe, England and Wales, more rarely in Scotland and Ireland.

Many **Sow-thistles** or Milk-thistles look like a cross between a thistle and a dandelion, but belong to the genus *Sonchus*. **Prickly Sow-thistle**, *S. asper*, and **Smooth Sow-thistle**, *S. oleraceus*, are common annual weeds of cultivated land, roadsides and waste places, found throughout the British Isles and much of Europe. They form branched, hollow stems up to 1.5m (5ft) tall. Prickly Sow-thistle has very prickly leaves, the lower ones with bases which curl around the stems, and few to several terminal flower heads. Smooth Sow-thistle has weakly spiny leaves, the lower ones with bases which clasp but do not curl around the stem, and numerous flower heads which are borne in a large, branching inflorescence.

Prickly
Sow-thistle
Sonchus asper

Smooth Sow-thistle
Sonchus oleraceus

Field Milk-thistle, *Sonchus arvensis*, is a similar but perennial plant, forming spreading colonies of erect stems up to 1.5m (5ft) tall with spiny-margined leaves, the lowermost lobed but the upper ones simple. It has open clusters of yellow flower heads, the stalks and involucres all covered with black, glandular hairs. This plant grows in a variety of places — in arable and waste land, beside streams, on the drift lines of brackish marshes, in sand-dunes and on shingle banks on the coasts across Europe and the British Isles.

Field Milk-thistle
Sonchus arvensis

Daisy family

Hawkweeds, *Hieracium* species, are a huge group, with somewhere between 10,000 and 20,000 species, mainly from temperate and Arctic regions of the northern hemisphere. They are perennial plants, either with most of their leaves in a basal rosette or with leafy, erect stems. Their flowers are borne in flower heads composed of ray florets, like those of dandelions, but each stem branches to carry several to many heads; most species have yellow flowers. Beneath each head the involucre is formed of bracts in overlapping rows.

Leafy Hawkweed
Hieracium umbellatum

Leafy Hawkweed, *Hieracium umbellatum*, grows in open woods, grassland and heaths throughout lowland areas of Europe and the British Isles. It has a slender, leafy stem up to 80cm (30in) tall, with many narrow, linear, slightly toothed leaves and a branched cluster of yellow flower heads. **Common Hawkweed**, *H. vulgatum*, by contrast, has a rosette of basal leaves and the flowering stem has only 2−4 leaves. The leaves are softly hairy, oblong to lance-shaped, often with toothed margins and purplish beneath. This is the commonest hawkweed in Scotland and northern England, growing in grassy and rocky places, woods and heaths; it is also found in Ireland, northern and central Europe.

Common Hawkweed
Hieracium vulgatum

Mouse-ear Hawkweed, *Hieracium pilosella*, forms spreading tufts of leaves each rosette producing creeping stems which form new plants at their tips. The leaves are usually lance-shaped and densely hairy beneath. The solitary, pale lemon-yellow flower heads grow on leafless, stiffly hairy, erect stems, often

Mouse-ear Hawkweed
Hieracium pilosella

only 15cm (6in) tall. The bracts of the involucre are covered in black-tipped hairs. Plants grow in dry, grassy places, on banks and walls, among rocks and in sand-dunes throughout Europe and much of the British Isles.

Hawk's-beards, *Crepis* species, are similar to hawkweeds, but there are only about 200 of them, mainly from Europe and Asia. **Smooth Hawk's-beard**, *C. capillaris*, is an annual plant found in grassland, waste places and roadsides, on walls and heaths throughout Europe and the British Isles. It has sinuately lobed leaves, the largest in a basal rosette, the stem leaves smaller and simpler. From each rosette grow one or more stems up to 90cm (3ft) tall, leafy near the base and branching to bear many yellow flower heads. The achenes which follow have parachutes formed of many rows of soft, white hairs. This last feature serves to distinguish *Crepis* from *Hieracium* species, for the achenes of the latter have one or two rows of brittle, pale brownish hairs.

Dandelions, *Taraxacum officinale*, are weeds found throughout temperate regions of the world, including Europe and the British Isles, growing in gardens, waste places, cultivated ground and roadsides, in grassland, on walls and sand-dunes. They have persistent tap roots and rosettes of wavy-lobed leaves, with solitary yellow flower heads in early summer, each one at the top of a hollow stalk. Both stalk and leaves exude milky juice if broken. The heads are followed by 'clocks' of parachuted seeds. Dandelion leaves can be added to salads, the roots roasted and ground to make a caffeine-free coffee substitute, and the flowers made into wine.

Smooth
Hawk's-beard
Crepis capillaris

Dandelion
Taraxacum officinalis

Flowering Rush family

Butomaceae The only species in this family is **Flowering Rush**, *Butomus umbellatus*, an uncommon plant found in ditches and ponds, or beside canals and slow-moving rivers throughout Europe, England and Ireland, rarely in Wales. It is a perennial with linear, twisted, three-angled leaves; on separate stems grow terminal umbels of flowers. Each bloom has six pink perianth segments, nine red stamens and six carpels. The fruits are reddish-purple follicles.

Flowering Rush
Butomus umbellatus

Common Water-plantain
Alisma plantago-aquatica

Water-plantain family

Alismataceae About 13 genera and 90 species of herbs, aquatic or from wet places, mainly of temperate and tropical regions of the northern hemisphere.

Family features Flowers regular, usually hermaphrodite. Perianth segments 6, free, in 2 whorls, the outer 3 green and sepal-like, inner 3 petal-like, soon falling. Stamens usually 3–6; ovary superior, of many free carpels. Fruit a cluster of achenes. Leaves long-stalked, often basal with open sheathing bases, often with arrow-shaped blades.

Common Water-plantain, *Alisma plantago-aquatica*, is found throughout Europe and much of the British Isles at the edges of ponds, slow-moving streams and ditches. It forms clumps of long-stalked leaves with elliptical or ovate blades; in early summer its branched flowering stalks grow 1m (3ft tall to bear umbel-like clusters of small white or pale pink flowers, followed by disk-like, flattened fruits borne in rings

Arrowhead, *Sagittaria sagittifolia*, grows at the edges of ponds, slow-moving rivers and ditches, scattered throughout much of the British Isles and Europe. It is a perennial, with clumps of long-stalked, arrow-shaped leaves; in summer its unbranched flowering stalks grow up to 90cm (3ft) tall and bear whorls of white, purple-blotched flowers, male flowers near the top, the smaller female flowers lower down and followed by heads of dark, flattened achenes.

Arrowhead
Sagittaria sagittifolia

Frogbit family

Hydrocharitaceae About 16 genera and 80 species of aquatic plants, mainly from warmer parts of the world.

   Family features Flowers regular, often unisexual, borne in a spathe. Perianth segments 6, outer 3 sepal-like and inner 3 petal-like (or inner ones 0); stamens 1 to many; ovary inferior with 1 cell. Fruits dry or fleshy. Leaves in rosettes or on stems.

Frogbit, *Hydrocharis morsus-ranae*, is a small plant with floating rosettes of long-stalked, round-bladed leaves. The small white flowers appear in the latter half of summer, males and females on separate plants. Frogbit grows in ponds, lakes and ditches scattered across Europe and the British Isles, except Scotland.

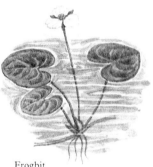

Frogbit
Hydrocharis morsus-ranae

Canadian Pondweed, *Elodea canadensis*, was introduced as an oxygenating plant for ponds and is now naturalized in still and slow-moving waters throughout most of the British Isles, in western and central Europe. This submerged plant has long stems and whorls of dark green, translucent leaves, usually borne in threes.

Canadian Pondweed
Elodea canadensis

Lily family

Liliaceae A large family of about 240 genera and 3000 species, mostly herbs, found throughout the world. Onions, garlic and leeks belong to this family. Garden plants include lilies, tulips, hyacinths, red hot pokers and hostas. Aloes are a source of the drug aloes, used as a laxative and in skin creams.

Family features Flowers usually regular and hermaphrodite. Perianth segments 6, usually petal-like, free or partly fused and in 2 distinct but similar whorls; stamens 6, opposite perianth segments; ovary superior with 3 cells. Fruit a capsule or fleshy berry. Leaves basal, alternate or whorled. The plants have rhizomes, corms or bulbs.

Scottish Asphodel, *Tofieldia pusilla*, is a small plant with sword-like leaves borne in two opposite rows so that they resemble a fan. In summer the flowering stems grow 20cm (8in) tall at most, each with a spike of greenish-white flowers, followed by globular capsules. Plants grow beside water in mountain meadows and among rocks in northern Europe and Scotland, in high mountains in France and Germany.

Bog Asphodel, *Narthecium ossifragum*, grows in wet, acid heaths, moors and *Sphagnum* bogs in western Europe, mainly in northern and western areas of the British Isles. It has fans of curved, sword-like leaves and erect flowering stems up to 45cm (18in) tall in the latter half of summer, with terminal racemes of yellow flowers. They have distinctive stamens, their filaments covered with dense yellow hairs and orange anthers. The plant is most obvious as the capsules ripen, for both capsules and stems become deep orange.

Scottish Asphodel
Tofieldia pusilla

Bog Asphodel
Narthecium ossifragum

White False Helleborine, *Veratrum album*, is a very poisonous plant causing symptoms similar to a heart attack. It is a stout perennial, with clumps of leafy stems up to 1.5m (5ft) tall and broad, alternate, strongly veined leaves. In the latter half of summer the branched stems bear many clusters of star-shaped flowers, hairy and greenish outside, white within. Plants grow in damp meadows and pastures in hills and mountains across much of Europe, but not in the British Isles.

Lily-of-the-valley, *Convallaria majalis*, grows in dry woods, mainly on calcareous soils, throughout much of Europe, mainly in England in the British Isles. It forms clumps of 2–4 leaves, the sheathing stalks of the leaves wrapped around each other to resemble a single stem. From the axils of some of these leaves the flowering stems grow in late spring; each one bears a drooping, one-sided spray of fragrant white bells followed by red berries. Lily-of-the-valley contains convallaramin, a drug which can be used as a less powerful heart tonic than digitalin, the active ingredient in Foxglove.

There are several species of Solomon's Seal in the genus *Polygonatum*.
Common Solomon's Seal, *P. multiflorum*, grows in woods, usually on calcareous soils, locally across much of Europe, mainly in southern England, south Wales and Cumbria in Great Britain, but also as a garden escape in other areas. This is a perennial plant with arching stems up to 80cm (30in) tall and alternate, broadly elliptical leaves. In the leaf axils hang small clusters of white, green-tipped, narrowly bell-shaped flowers followed by blue-black berries.

White False Helleborine
Veratrum album

Lily-of-the-valley
Convallaria majalis

Common
Solomon's Seal
Polygonatum multiflorum

Lily family

Wild Asparagus
Asparagus officinalis

Wild Asparagus, *Asparagus officinalis*, grows in woods and hedgerows, in waste places, in sand-dunes and on cliffs near the sea (where it is often found as a prostrate form) throughout Europe, naturalized in many places in Britain, mainly in England. This perennial plant has smooth, erect stems up to 1.5m (5ft) tall, much-branched and apparently bearing numerous clusters of needle-like leaves; however, these 'leaves' are actually reduced stems and the true leaves are the papery scales at the base of the 'leaf' clusters. Asparagus plants may be male or female, the flowers borne in the axils of the true leaves; the flowers are bell-like, males yellow and females yellow-green, followed by red berries. Young shoots of wild plants can be eaten like those of cultivated forms.

Butcher's Broom, *Ruscus aculeatus*, is a small shrub with branched green stems up to 80cm (30in) tall and apparently with thick, dark green, spine-pointed leaves, each one twisted at the base. But, as in Asparagus, these 'leaves' are reduced stems and the true leaves are small, papery scales, one at the base of each false leaf. Plants may be male or female, one small greenish flower borne on the surface of each false leaf, cupped in a membranous bract. Female flowers are followed by red berries. This plant grows in woods and dry, rocky places in western Europe, mainly in southern England and southwest Wales in Britain. It is also grown in gardens and has escaped to grow wild in other areas.

Butcher's Broom
Ruscus aculeatus

Martagon Lily
Lilium martagon

The true Lilies are a group of about 90 *Lilium* species, around nine of which are found in Europe. The **Martagon**

Lily, *L. martagon*, grows in woods and mountain pastures across much of Europe, except in the north; in England it is often grown in gardens and is also found wild in several woodland localities. It forms an erect stem up to 1m (3ft) tall, with whorls of ovate or lance-shaped leaves and a raceme of nodding flowers at the top of the stem in late summer. The flowers are pink or pale purple with darker spots on the inside and strongly recurved petals. The protruding stamens have versatile, reddish-brown anthers.

Fritillaries are bulbous plants belonging to the genus *Fritillaria*. Some are large, striking plants, like the Imperial Fritillaries grown in gardens, but others are small and delicate, like the native **Snake's-head Fritillary**, *F. meleagris*. This species grows in damp meadows and pastures across most of Europe, mainly in southern England in Britain and not in Ireland. It has disappeared in many areas with the eradication of the water meadows. In spring a single stem grows from each bulb, reaching about 30cm (1ft) tall and bearing several linear leaves and one nodding flower at the top. The flower is like a lantern, with six petals chequered in light and dark purple.

Snake's-head Fritillary
Fritillaria meleagris

Snowdon Lily, *Lloydia serotina*, grows on ledges, among rocks and in pastures in the mountains of central Europe but only in Snowdonia in Britain. It is a small bulbous plant, with two or more thread-like leaves and an erect flowering stem 15cm (6in) tall at most; this bears several linear leaves and a single flower around midsummer. The flower is bell-shaped with six white, red-veined petals persisting beneath the globular capsule as it enlarges.

Snowdon Lily
Lloydia serotina

Lily family

Star-of-Bethlehem
*Ornithogalum
umbellatum*

Drooping
Star-of-Bethlehem
*Ornithogalum
nutans*

Spring Squill
Scilla verna

Star-of-Bethlehem, *Ornithogalum umbellatum*, has many white bulbs and produces grassy, white-striped leaves in spring, together with flowering stems up to 30cm (1ft) tall, their starry, white flowers borne in flat-topped, terminal racemes. The backs of their petals are green-striped. The species is often grown in gardens but also grows wild in grassy places and cultivated land across much of Europe, except the north; it has probably been introduced into Great Britain but is now widespread.

Drooping Star-of-Bethlehem, *Ornithogalum nutans*, comes originally from the Mediterranean region but is naturalized in grassy places elsewhere in Europe, including eastern and central England. In spring its egg-shaped bulbs produce white-striped, grass-like leaves and erect flowering stems up to 60cm (2ft) tall, with one-sided racemes of white flowers. There is a wide green band down the outside of each petal. The stamens have broad filaments cleft at the tips with anthers in the clefts. Over 20 *Ornithogalum* species grow in Europe, all with basal leaves and white, starry flowers marked with green.

Spring Squill, *Scilla verna*, is one of about 80 *Scilla* species, over 20 of which occur in Europe. It is a small bulbous plant, with a tuft of grass-like leaves appearing in spring before the flowering stems; these bear flat-topped clusters of starry, blue-violet flowers held more or less erect. Plants grow in dry, grassy places and heaths in western Europe, very locally in the British Isles, mainly on the west coast of Great Britain, in the Hebrides and on the east coast of Ireland.

In late spring **Bluebells**, *Hyacinthoides non-scripta*, form blue carpets in oak woods, also in hedges and sometimes in heathland, throughout western Europe and the British Isles, but their numbers are declining with the disappearance of woods and heaths. Bluebells have white bulbs and linear, grass-like leaves. Mature bulbs also produce violet-blue flowers borne in drooping, one-sided racemes on leafless stalks up to 50cm (20in) tall. The flowers are narrowly bell-shaped with recurved tips, nodding when open but with erect buds. They are followed by three-lobed capsules.

Herb Paris, *Paris quadrifolia*, has erect stems about 30cm (1ft) tall, each with a whorl of four glossy leaves halfway up and a single starry flower at the top, appearing in summer. This flower has four (sometimes more) broad green sepals, four thread-like green petals and six prominent, erect stamens. At the centre of the flower the fleshy, globular capsule develops, turning black when ripe. Plants are scattered in damp woods on calcareous soils across most of Europe, mainly in England in Great Britain and absent from many western areas and Ireland. They are poisonous.

Autumn Crocus, *Colchicum autumnale*, is also known as Meadow Saffron and Naked Ladies. Its flowers are like pale purple goblets with orange anthers, appearing in autumn from corms buried in the soil. When the flowers die back they leave developing capsules at soil level. The large, glossy leaves appear in the spring. This plant grows in damp meadows and woods across most of Europe, in England and eastern Wales and a few places in southeastern Ireland. It is extremely poisonous.

Bluebell
Hyacinthoides non-scripta

Herb Paris
Paris quadrifolia

Autumn Crocus
Colchicum autumnale

Lily family

Onions are a group of about 700 species in the genus *Allium*, found throughout the northern hemisphere and Africa, with 90 in Europe. They are all more or less scented plants; some, like onions, chives, leeks and garlic, are eaten as vegetables. These are bulbous plants, their flowers borne in terminal umbels, each umbel enclosed in a spathe in bud. Some species produce bulbils as well as flowers in their umbels.

Ramsons, *Allium ursinum*, is found in damp woods, hedgerows and other shady places throughout Europe and the British Isles. It forms carpets of elliptical, garlic-scented leaves growing from narrow, solitary bulbs in spring and early summer, two leaves and one flowering stem from each bulb. The white, starry flowers are borne in flat-topped umbels, each with a membranous spathe, growing on angled stems about 30cm (1ft) tall.

Triquetrous Garlic, *Allium triquetrum*, has small, whitish bulbs and three-angled stems and leaves. The stems grow up to 50cm (20in) tall and bear one-sided umbels of bell-shaped, white flowers with green lines on the petals. Plants grow beside streams, in damp woods and hedgerows in Spain and France. They have been introduced into southwestern England and the Channel Islands, and to a few places in south Wales and southern Ireland.

Crow Garlic, *Allium vineale*, grows in dry, grassy places, fields, vineyards and roadsides throughout Europe; it has been introduced into the British Isles, becoming a weed in some parts of eastern England and the Midlands. It

Ramsons
Allium ursinum

Triquetrous Garlic
Allium triquetrum

has erect stems up to 60cm (2ft) tall,
sheathed by linear leaves. Its umbels
produce purple bulbils as well as pink
or greenish-white flowers, sometimes
bulbils only.

Daffodil family

Amaryllidaceae About 85 genera and
1100 species of bulbous plants, the
majority from warm temperate regions.
Ornamental plants in the family include
daffodils, snowdrops and hippeastrums.
  Family features Flowers solitary or
in umbels, enclosed in a membranous
spathe in bud; hermaphrodite, usually
regular. Perianth segments 6, in 2
whorls, sometimes with a corona;
stamens 6, in 2 whorls opposite the
perianth segments; ovary inferior with 3
cells. Fruits usually capsules. These are
bulbous plants with basal leaves.

Crow Garlic
Allium vineale

Snowdrops, *Galanthus nivalis*, grow
beside streams, in damp woods, hedgerows and meadows throughout much of
Europe and Great Britain, except the
north. They form small clumps of
linear, grey-green leaves in late winter,
together with flowering stems bearing
solitary, nodding flowers. Each flower
has three spreading white, outer
perianth segments and three smaller,
green-spotted, inner perianth segments.

Snowdrop
*Galanthus
nivalis*

About 40 *Narcissus* species are found in
Europe. **Wild Daffodils**, *N.
pseudonarcissus*, grow in damp woods
and meadows, orchards and roadsides
across much of Europe, locally in
England and Wales. Their broad, linear
leaves grow from bulbs in spring, with
leafless flowering stems and solitary,
drooping flowers. Each flower has a
spreading, pale yellow perianth and a
deep yellow corona (the trumpet).

Wild Daffodil
Narcissus pseudonarcissus

Iris family

Iridaceae About 60 genera and 800 species of herbs, found worldwide. Garden plants include irises, crocuses and montbretias. Freesias and gladioli make superb cut flowers.

Family features Flowers hermaphrodite, usually regular with 1 or 2 bracts forming a spathe. Perianth segments 6, in 2 whorls of 3 (alike in both whorls or dissimilar); stamens 3, opposite the outer perianth segments; ovary inferior with 3 cells. Fruits are capsules. The plants have rhizomes, bulbs or corms. They form clumps of flattened, linear leaves folded and overlapping at the base, sheathing the bases of the flowering stems.

Irises are a group of about 300 species in the genus *Iris*, found across temperate regions of the northern hemisphere. About 50 grow wild in Europe and others in gardens. They are perennial plants with clumps of sword-shaped, overlapping leaves and separate flowering stems with terminal flower clusters. Iris flowers are showy, with three clawed, outer perianth segments flexed downwards (the 'falls'), three clawed inner segments (the 'standards'), which are usually erect, and bearded in some species, and a three-cleft style (the 'crest'), with three petal-like sections arching over the stamens.

Yellow Flag, *Iris pseudacorus*, grows beside rivers and ponds, in marshes, wet meadows and ditches throughout Europe and the British Isles. It has stiff erect leaves about 1m (3ft) tall growing from tangled rhizomes. Among the leaves grow the flowering stems, each with a cluster of yellow flowers in summer. Each flower has three broad,

Yellow Flag
Iris pseudacorus

Stinking Iris
Iris foetidissima

Blue-eyed Grass
Sisyrinchium bermudiana

hanging falls, three smaller, upright standards and three arching styles, ragged at their tips. They are followed by green capsules with brown seeds.

Stinking Iris or Gladdon, *Iris foetidissima*, has evergreen, sword-shaped leaves with an unpleasant scent when crushed. The flowering stems bear purple flowers tinged or veined with yellow, the standards shorter than the falls and more yellow. They are followed by brownish capsules with orange seeds.

Blue-eyed Grass, *Sisyrinchium bermudiana*, is a perennial with tufts of overlapping leaves, 50cm (20in) tall at most. The flowering stems bear umbels of blue flowers with yellow centres, each with six identical perianth segments. Plants are grown in gardens but in the wild are found only in marshy meadows and on lake shores in western Ireland.

Crocuses, *Crocus* species, are popular garden plants, their goblet-like flowers most familiar in spring. However, **Autumn Crocus**, *C. nudiflorus*, produces its purple flowers in early autumn quite separately from the white-striped leaves which appear in spring. Both grow from corms beneath the soil. Plants grow in grassy meadows and heaths in France and Spain, becoming naturalized in a few places in England.

Wild Gladiolus, *Gladiolus illyricus*, grows in bushy places, heaths and marshes in southern and western Europe, very locally in the New Forest and the Isle of Wight in England. It grows from corms, producing erect tufts of sword-like leaves and one-sided spikes of crimson-purple flowers.

Autumn Crocus
Crocus nudiflorus

Wild Gladiolus
Gladiolus illyricus

Yam family

Dioscoreaceae A family of twining vines, with 8–9 genera and about 750 species, found in tropical and warm temperate regions of the world.

Black Bryony, *Tamus communis*, is the only widespread species in Europe, found across much of the Continent, in England and Wales, on fences, in woodland edges and hedgerows. It is a perennial plant with twining stems, 2–4m (6–12ft) long; the stems are smooth and angular, unbranched with pointed heart-shaped, shiny leaves. The flowers are yellowish-green with six perianth segments and borne in the leaf axils. Plants may be male or female, male flowers on long stalks in elongated clusters, females in smaller, shorter clusters on short, recurved stalks. Female flowers are followed by berries, green at first and ripening bright red, poisonous like the rest of the plant.

Black Bryony
Tamus communis

Bur-reed family

Sparganiaceae Only one genus and about 20 species of aquatic plants, found in many parts of the world.

Bur-reeds, *Sparganium* species, are perennial plants found in marshes or in shallow water on the edges of ponds and slow-moving rivers, where they may form extensive stands. They have erect or floating stems and narrow, grass-like leaves, the bases of the leaves sheathing the stems. Their flowers are borne in small green balls, male flowers near the tip of the stem, females below.

Branched Bur-reed
Sparganium erectum

Branched Bur-reed, *Sparganium erectum*, varies in height, often growing 30–60cm (1–2ft) but sometimes up to

2m (6ft) tall. It forms clumps of erect, three-angled leaves and branched flowering stems in the latter half of summer. Balls of male flowers are borne above the females on the branches. Plants grow in ponds and marshes, slow-moving rivers and ditches throughout much of Europe and the British Isles.

Bulrush family

Typhaceae Only one genus, *Typha*, and 10 species, found throughout the world. All are aquatic plants, growing in marshes and reed-beds, on the edges of ponds and slow-moving rivers, and in ditches. They are large perennial plants with erect stems up to 2.5m (9ft) tall and thick, sword-like, overlapping leaves. The stiff, unbranched stems bear the flowers in terminal, cylindrical heads, the greenish female flowers below and male flowers above. Male flowers are shed after the pollen has gone, leaving a bare stalk, but female flowers go on to form brown fruiting heads which last for months.

Bulrush, *Typha latifolia*, grows up to 2.4m (9ft) tall, with leaves up to 20mm (¾in) across. Its male and female flowers form one continuous cylindrical flower spike. **Lesser Bulrush**, *T. angustifolia*, is usually not more than 2m (6ft) tall, with narrow leaves only 6mm (¼in) wide. Its male and female flowers are separated by a section of stem up to 8cm (3in) long. Both species are widespread in Europe north to southern Scandinavia, but Bulrush is common while Lesser Bulrush is much rarer. In the British Isles Bulrushes are common in England, Wales and Ireland, rare in Scotland; Lesser Bulrushes are scattered in England, rare in other areas.

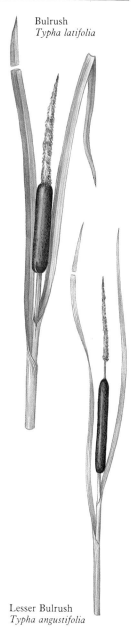

Bulrush
Typha latifolia

Lesser Bulrush
Typha angustifolia

Arum family

Araceae About 115 genera and 2000 species of herbs, mainly from the tropics, often found in jungles. Popular house plants in this family, like philodendrons and monsteras, are mostly grown for their impressive leaves.

Family features Flowers very small, often with an offensive scent, and borne in a dense spike (a spadix), usually subtended by a leafy spathe; unisexual or hermaphrodite. If unisexual, then male flowers borne on upper part of spadix, females below. Perianth usually present in hermaphrodite flowers, absent in unisexual flowers; stamens 2–8; ovary superior or embedded in spadix, with 1–3 cells. Fruit usually a berry, but may be leathery and split open. Leaves often with sheathing bases, usually in a basal clump. Plants contain acrid juice.

Sweetflag
Acorus calamus

Cuckoo-pint
Arum maculatum

Sweetflag, *Acorus calamus*, grows on the margins of slow-moving rivers and canals, ponds and lakes across much of Europe, except the north, mainly in England in the British Isles; it has been introduced from Asia. It has stout rhizomes and sword-like, wavy-edged leaves up to 1m (3ft) tall, with a scent of tangerines and cinnamon when bruised. The flowering stems resemble three-angled leaves and bear flower-spikes about halfway up, growing at an angle of about 45 degrees to the stems and packed with unpleasantly scented, yellowish, hermaphrodite flowers. The rhizomes yield an oil used in perfumery; they are also used in herb medicine and the production of Stockton Bitters.

Cuckoo-pint or Lords-and-ladies, *Arum maculatum*, grows in hedgerows and woods throughout much of Europe and the British Isles, rarely in the north. The leaves unfurl in spring; they are shiny green, often black-spotted, arrow-shaped with long stalks. They are followed by the spathe — pale yellow-green and edged or streaked with purple — containing the dull purple spadix. After pollination, spathe and leaves wither, leaving green berries at the top of a bare stalk; these turn red by late summer. They are very poisonous and the whole plant contains acrid sap.

Duckweed family

Lemnaceae A small family of floating aquatic plants, with 3 genera and about 40 species, found in fresh water throughout the world.

Duckweeds, the *Lemna* species, are found in ponds and ditches. They have floating, leaf-like fronds (known as the thallus) and minute flowers which lack petals or sepals. **Common Duckweed**, *L. minor*, has opaque, rounded thalli which constantly divide to form new ones; duckweeds spread rapidly. Each thallus has a single root beneath and may form flowers in a cavity on the upper surface if growing in shallow, sunlit water. This is the most common species, growing in ponds and ditches throughout Europe, much of Great Britain and Ireland.

Ivy-leaved Duckweed, *Lemna trisulca*, is a submerged species, floating just beneath the surface of the water in ponds and ditches throughout Europe and much of the British Isles. Its thalli are translucent and pointed-oval in shape; they float in clumps, several thalli joined together by their stalks, new ones arising in opposite pairs and at right angles to the parent.

Common Duckweed
Lemna minor

Ivy-leaved Duckweed
Lemna trisulca

Orchid family

Orchidaceae One of the largest plant families, with about 735 genera and 17,000 species known to date. Many are found in temperate regions of the world, but far more grow in tropical jungles and more are found every year.

Family features Flowers solitary, or borne in a spike or raceme; hermaphrodite, bilaterally symmetrical. Perianth segments 6, in 2 whorls; often the whorls are unlike, the outer one sepal-like and inner one petal-like. Often the central sepal becomes the uppermost part of the flower; the sides are formed by 2 lateral sepals and 2 lateral petals, and the central petal hangs downwards, forming the lip. Stamens 1 or 2, their anthers borne with the stigmas on a structure known as the column. Ovary inferior, usually with 1 cell. Fruit usually a capsule with numerous minute seeds. Leaves entire, usually in 2 overlapping rows at the base of the stem or alternate, often fleshy, with a sheathing base encircling the stem, sometimes reduced to scales.

Three **Lady's-slipper Orchids**, *Cypripedium* species, grow in Europe, out of a world total of about 50, many of them now rare. **Yellow Lady's-slipper**, *C. calceolus*, has an erect stem up to 45cm (18in) tall, appearing in early summer and bearing 3–4 large, elliptical leaves with one (sometimes two) flowers at the tip. The flower has wavy purple sepals, one erect at the top and the two lateral ones joined and pointing downwards, two purple, spirally twisted lateral petals and a yellow pouched lip spotted with red inside. At one time this plant grew in many woodland localities in Europe and in several places in northern England,

Yellow Lady's-slipper
Cypripedium calceolus

Marsh Helleborine
Epipactis palustris

in hills and mountains, usually in calcareous soils. It has been eradicated in many places and only one small colony is left in England.

Several Helleborines, *Epipactis* species, grow in Europe and the British Isles. **Marsh Helleborine**, *E. palustris*, grows in fens and marshes, wet meadows and dune slacks locally across most of Europe, in England, Wales and Ireland. It has a slender stem up to 45cm (18in) tall and oblong to lance-shaped, often purplish leaves, their bases clasping the stem. The flowers are borne in a terminal, more or less one-sided raceme, each in the axil of a narrow, pointed bract. They have purplish-green sepals, smaller, whitish lateral petals veined with purple at the base, and a frilly white lip veined with pink and spotted with yellow.

Broad-leaved Helleborine, *Epipactis helleborine*, has an erect stem up to 80cm (30in) tall, broadly ovate leaves and dull purple or greenish flowers. Usually the sepals are greenish, the petals are purple and the lip purple or greenish-white, darker green or brown inside. Plants grow in woods and rocky places throughout Europe and much of the British Isles.

White Helleborine, *Cephalanthera damasonium*, has a leafy stem up to 50cm (20in) tall, ovate to lance-shaped leaves and large, leafy bracts near the top of the stem. The flowers are creamy-white, closed except for a brief time when they open into up-facing bells, petals and sepals curved around the yellow-blotched lip. This plant grows in calcareous soils, in woods and shady places scattered across Europe and in England in Britain.

Broad-leaved Helleborine
Epipactis helleborine

White Helleborine
Cephalanthera damasonium

Orchid family

Creeping Lady's Tresses, *Goodyera repens*, has creeping stems ending in rosettes of ovate, white-veined leaves. The flowering stems grow 25cm (10in) tall and bear spirally twisted racemes of creamy-white, fragrant flowers in the latter half of summer. Each flower grows in the axil of a large, linear bract which is green on the outside, white on the inside. The upper sepal and the two petals of each flower form a hood; the lateral sepals are spreading and the lip is flat and triangular. This rather rare orchid grows in mossy coniferous woods in hills and mountains across much of Europe; it is found locally in East Anglia and the north of England, more frequently in northern Scotland.

The Lady's Tresses, *Spiranthes* species, are small orchids with leafy, erect stems and spirally twisted racemes of flowers. **Autumn Lady's Tresses**, *S. spiralis*, grows in damp, grassy places, meadows and pastures, on sand-dunes and hills, usually in calcareous soils, throughout much of Europe, except the north, in England, Wales and Ireland. It produces a rosette of elliptical or ovate leaves in late summer, then an erect flowering stem in late summer of the following year. By this time the leaves have withered but a new rosette has formed to one side. The flowering stem grows about 30cm (1ft tall), has overlapping scale leaves near the base and a single twisted row of scented, white flowers at the top.

Twayblade, *Listera ovata*, flowers in the early part of summer. It has a slender, erect flowering stem up to 60cm (2ft) tall with a pair of rounded, ovate-elliptical, almost opposite leaves

Creeping Lady's Tresses
Goodyera repens

Autumn Lady's Tresses
Spiranthes spirales

towards the base. The numerous yellow-green flowers are small and spurless, borne in a slender raceme terminating the stem. The petals and sepals are joined at the base to form an open hood over the long, dangling lip; this has a deep notch at the tip.

Violet Bird's-nest Orchid, *Limodorum abortivum*, is one of several unrelated saprophytic orchids which have lost their chlorophyll. They usually grow in leaf litter in shady woods and they depend on the mycorrhiza in their roots to absorb water and nutrients from this leafy humus. This species grows in woods across much of Europe, except the north, but not in the British Isles. The flowering stems appear at unpredictable intervals, growing up to 80cm (30in) tall, with several scale leaves and a terminal raceme of flowers, all violet in colour. The flowers have spreading lateral sepals and petals, a helmet-shaped upper sepal, a yellow-tinged lip and a downward-pointing spur.

Bird's-nest Orchid, *Neottia nidus-avis*, is another saprophytic species found only in shady woodland, particularly beneath beech, throughout much of Europe, Great Britain and Ireland, most commonly in the south. It has a ball of thick, fleshy roots concealing its rhizome (the 'bird's nest'), buried in leaf litter on the woodland floor; the plant only appears above ground when it flowers. It has a stiff erect, brownish flowering stem up to 45cm (18in) tall, with many membranous, brown scale leaves and a dense spike of brown flowers. Each one has sepals and petals joined into an open hood and a long, dangling, lobed lip, pouched at the base and often darker than the rest of the flower.

Twayblade
Listera ovata

Violet Bird's-nest Orchid
Limodorum abortivum

Bird's-nest Orchid
Neottia nidus-avis

Orchid family

Coral-root
*Corallorhiza
trifida*

Bog Orchid
*Hammarbya
paludosa*

Frog Orchid
Coeloglossum viride

Coral-root, *Corallorhiza trifida*, is a partly saprophytic plant, with a fleshy, branched rhizome resembling a piece of coral. It grows in damp, mossy woods, often beneath pine or alder, also in dune slacks, scattered across much of Europe, in northern England and Scotland; its presence can only be detected when it flowers. Often several stems are produced, growing 25cm (10in) tall at most. They are yellow-green with brown-veined, sheathing scale leaves near the base and a few flowers at the top. The sepals and lateral petals are yellow-green, the lip whitish and spotted with crimson.

Bog Orchid, *Hammarbya paludosa*, is a tiny species 12cm (5in) tall at most. It has a rosette of shiny, rounded leaves, their margins often fringed with tiny bulbils, and a spike of minute, yellow-green flowers. Each flower has spreading petals and sepals and a lip that points upwards. Plants grow in wet *Sphagnum* bogs in northern and central Europe, mainly in Scotland in the British Isles. At one time the species was more widespread but it has disappeared with its wetland habitats.

Frog Orchid, *Coeloglossum viride*, has a flowering stem about 25cm (10in) tall, with several brownish sheaths at its base and several leaves, the lowermost large and rounded, upper ones smaller and narrower. The slightly scented, small flowers are borne in a cylindrical spike; each has a hood of greenish or brownish sepals, green lateral petals often hidden by the hood, and a dangling green lip, three-lobed near the tip and tinged with reddish-brown. This plant grows in calcareous grassland, usually in hills and mountains, sometimes in dunes or on rock ledges, scattered across most of Europe and the British Isles, more commonly in the north.

Fragrant Orchid, *Gymnadenia conopsea*, grows up to 40cm (15in) tall and its leaves are narrow, lower ones lance-shaped and slightly hooded, upper ones pressed close to the stem. The flowers are vanilla-scented, often reddish-lilac, sometimes white or purple, borne in a dense, cylindrical spike. Each has a hood, two spreading lateral petals, a rounded, three-lobed lip and a long, slender, often curved spur. Fragrant Orchids usually grow in grassland on calcareous soils, but also in heaths and woods; one variety grows in fens and marshes. They are found throughout Europe and much of the British Isles.

Fragrant Orchid
Gymnadenia conopsea

Butterfly Orchids are a group of about 200 species in the genus *Platanthera*, but few are found in Europe. **Greater Butterfly Orchid**, *P. chlorantha*, has an erect stem up to 40cm (15in) tall, two bluntly elliptical basal leaves and a rather pyramidal spike of greenish flowers, sweetly scented at night; each bloom has spreading lateral sepals, the upper sepal and lateral petals joined into a hood, and a strap-shaped lip with a long, slender spur. Plants grow in woods and grassland, often on calcareous soils, scattered throughout much of Europe and the British Isles. Lesser Butterfly Orchid, *P. bifolia*, is similar but smaller, with a more cylindrical spike of whitish, less scented flowers. It grows in wet moors and heaths, often in calcareous flushes, also in grassland and woods, scattered throughout Europe and much of the British Isles.

Greater Butterfly Orchid
Platanthera chlorantha

Orchid family

Musk Orchid
Herminium monorchis

Lizard Orchid
Himantoglossum hircinum

Musk Orchid, *Herminium monorchis*, has two elliptical-oblong leaves and a flowering stem about 15cm (6in) tall; this has a small scale leaf halfway up and ends in a cylindrical spike of small, greenish, fragrant flowers, formed of spreading petals and sepals and a three-lobed lip. This rare plant grows in short grassland, on chalk or limestone, scattered across much of Europe and England. Its numbers have declined rapidly in recent years with the conversion of the downs and limestone hills from sheep grazing to arable land.

Lizard Orchid, *Himantoglossum hircinum*, has a stout stem usually about 40cm (15in) tall with oblong-elliptical leaves. The untidy-looking flowers are borne in a loose spike and smell of stale perspiration. Each has a grey-green hood formed of sepals and lateral petals, often streaked with purple, and a three-lobed lip, with curly lateral lobes and a long, undulating central lobe, furry and whitish at the base with purple spots, and brownish-green towards the end, notched at the tip. This lobe is coiled like a spring in bud. This orchid is rare; it grows in woodland margins and clearings, on roadside verges and in grassland, usually on chalk and limestone, scattered across Europe, except in the north, mainly in southeastern England in Great Britain.

The *Ophrys* species are a group of about 30 orchids, many with flowers resembling insects or spiders; the majority come from the Mediterranean region. **Bee Orchid**, *O. apifera*, has elliptical leaves, a stem 45cm (18in) tall at most and a spike of 2–5 flowers around midsummer. Each flower has three broad sepals, pink or white on the inside, green on the back, two small, lance-shaped, pinkish-green lateral petals, and a lip that looks like a bumblebee. The lip is three-lobed; the two lateral lobes are small and hairy and the central lobe is globular, dark brown and velvety, with two yellow spots and a pointed tip that curves backwards. Bee Orchids grow in grassland, on the edges of fields, on roadsides and in quarries, often on chalk and limestone, also in fixed dunes and on clay soils. They are scattered across much of Europe, except the north, in England, Wales and Ireland; their numbers are decreasing.

Early Spider Orchid, *Ophrys sphegodes*, has flowers that resemble spiders, borne in a spike of 2–8 flowers in spring and early summer; their sepals are green, their petals yellow-green and the rounded lip dark velvety brown with a bluish H- or X-shaped cross. This orchid grows in short grassland on chalk or limestone scattered across much of Europe, except the north, and in southern England; its numbers have decreased rapidly in recent years.

Fly Orchid, *Ophrys insectifera*, grows up to 60cm (2ft) tall, with an elongated spike of 4–12 flowers. Each bloom has oblong, yellow-green sepals, purple-brown, velvety, thread-like petals and a narrow, three-lobed lip like a fly. The lip is velvety brown with a broad, bluish band across the middle, two small lateral lobes and a notched tip. Fly Orchids are not as rare as Spider Orchids, but are not common. They grow in woods and coppices, on grassy banks, in fields and on roadsides, sometimes in fens, usually on calcareous soils, across much of Europe, in England, parts of Wales and central Ireland.

Bee Orchid
Ophrys apifera

Early Spider
Orchid
Ophrys sphegodes

Fly Orchid
Ophrys insectifera

Orchid family

About 22 orchids from the genus *Orchis* grow in Europe. In some species the sepals and petals of the flower form a hood over the column, in others the lateral sepals are spreading; the lip is usually three-lobed and spurred.

In many *Orchis* species the lip looks like a man, with two lateral lobes near the base (the arms), and a central lobe forked near the tip (to form the legs); often there is a little 'tooth' between the legs. The **Lady Orchid**, *O. purpurea*, is a rare orchid most often found in open woods on calcareous soils, across much of Europe, except the north, in Kent and Sussex in Britain. It has a flowering stem about 40cm (15in) tall, shiny, ovate leaves and a dense flower spike in early summer. Each bloom grows in the axil of a membranous bract (this is true of all *Orchis* species), has a dark reddish-purple helmet and a white lip flushed with rose-pink and spotted with reddish-purple. The flowers are fragrant and the leaves smell of coumarin (new-mown hay) as they die.

The **Burnt-tip Orchid**, *Orchis ustulata*, gets its name from the darkness of the dark maroon flower buds at the tip of the spike. Open flowers look lighter, with a dark purple helmet and a white, man-shaped lip spotted with red-purple. This is another relatively rare orchid, scattered in short grassland over chalk and limestone across the hills and mountains of Europe and found in England. It forms a rosette of elliptical leaves, with a stout stem up to 20cm (8in) tall and a dense spike of flowers in early summer. The flowers smell of heliotrope and the dying leaves of new-mown hay.

Lady Orchid
Orchis purpurea

Burnt-tip Orchid
Orchis ustulata

Early Purple Orchid, *Orchis mascula*, is common in open woods and grassland throughout most of Europe and the British Isles. It forms rosettes of bluntly lance-shaped leaves, black-spotted like those of a Spotted Orchid, and has an erect flowering stem up to 60cm (2ft) tall. The flowers vary from pale pink to bright purple; they have a helmet formed from the upper sepal and petals but the lateral sepals spread out at first and then fold back. The lip is three-lobed and about as broad as long. At first the flowers are vanilla-scented, but the scent acquires a hint of tom-cats after pollination.

The flowers of the **Green-winged Orchid**, *Orchis morio*, have spreading helmets marked with green veins and folded over reddish-purple, three-lobed lips. Its flowering spike grows up to 40cm (15in) tall and its leaves are elliptical. This common orchid is found in grassy places, meadows and pastures, on banks and roadside verges, often on calcareous soils, across most of Europe, in lowland areas of England and Wales, and in central Ireland.

Pyramidal Orchid, *Anacamptis pyramidalis*, is one of the commonest European orchids found on chalk or limestone, in grassland, open scrub and woodland throughout most of Europe, in the British Isles north to southern Scotland. Its flowering spike is pyramidal when young, becoming cylindrical as more flowers open. The flowers are scented, deep rose-purple, with spreading lateral sepals, a hood formed of the other sepal and petals, and a broad, three-lobed lip with a long, slender spur. The leafy flowering stem grows about 45cm (18in) tall, its leaves narrowly lance-shaped and keeled.

Early Purple
Orchid
Orchis mascula

Green-winged
Orchid
Orchis morio

Pyramidal Orchid
Anacamptis pyramidalis

Orchid family

Marsh and **Spotted Orchids** are a group of about 30 species in the genus *Dactylorhiza*. In their flowers the lateral sepals are always spreading, never contributing to the helmet often formed by the upper sepal and petals.

Early Marsh Orchid
Dactylorhiza incarnata

Common Spotted Orchid
Dactylorhiza fuchsii

Early Marsh Orchid, *Dactylorhiza incarnata*, has a flowering stem about 60cm (2ft) tall, with several keeled, lance-shaped, erect leaves, hooded at their tips, and a dense, cylindrical spike of many flowers in summer; these are often flesh-coloured and marked with spots and lines of darker colour, but they vary from pale yellow to magenta-purple. The upper sepal and the petals fall forwards over the flower, the lip has a short spur and its margins are turned backwards. This orchid grows in marshes and wet meadows, peaty fens and bogs, sometimes in dune slacks, scattered across most of Europe and the British Isles.

Spotted Orchids, members of the two species *Dactylorhiza fuchsii* and *D. maculata*, are recognizable from the dark spots on their leaves. They are among the most common European orchids. **Common Spotted Orchid**, *D. fuchsii*, often forms large colonies in open woods and scrub, in short grassland, often in calcareous soils, also in marshes and stabilized sand-dunes throughout much of Europe and the British Isles. Its leaves are keeled and marked with elongated, often confluent dark spots. The flowers are borne in spikes which are conical when young, becoming cylindrical as they age; they vary from white to reddish-purple but are always marked with a symmetrical pattern of lines and blotches. Each flower has spreading lateral sepals, a helmet formed of the upper sepal and the petals, and a spurred, three-lobed lip. The narrow central lobe of the lip is longer than the rounder lateral lobes.

Heath Spotted Orchid, *Dactylorhiza maculata*, has leaves with much smaller, lighter, rounded spots; the spots may even be faint or absent. The leaves are narrowly lance-shaped or linear, and the stem grows 15–50cm (6–20in) tall. Its pyramidal spikes have a few large flowers, usually pale lilac-pink marked with darker loops and dots, but varying to dark pink. The flowers have a lip that is broader than long, with its central lobe smaller than the lateral lobes. Plants grow in acid, peaty soils, in damp moors and dry heaths, oak and beech woods, and in grassland across Europe and much of the British Isles, most commonly in the north and west.

Marsh Orchids, subspecies of *Dactylorhiza majalis*, are found in wet places. They grow about 60cm (2ft) tall and their leaves vary from unspotted to heavily spotted. The flowers have upward-spreading lateral sepals (that look like wings), a helmet formed from the upper sepal and the lateral petals, and a lip which is broader than long.
Southern Marsh Orchid, *D. majalis* subsp. *praetermissa*, has pale magenta-red or rich lilac flowers; its leaves are often unmarked and it usually grows 40cm (18in) tall or more. It is found in marshes and fens, bogs, wet meadows and dune slacks, usually in calcareous soils, in northwest Europe, England and Wales. Northern Marsh Orchid, *D. majalis* subsp. *purpurella*, is smaller, with rich red-purple flowers. It is found in similar habitats in northern Europe and northern areas of the British Isles.

Heath Spotted Orchid
Dactylorhiza maculata

Southern Marsh Orchid
Dactylorhiza majalis
subsp. *praetermissa*

Glossary

Note: Where terms are specific to a family, they have been defined within the **Family features** of that family.

Achene A small, indehiscent, dry fruit with one seed. Its thin wall distinguishes it from a nutlet.

Alien An introduced plant which has become naturalized.

Alternate An arrangement of leaves on a stem, such that each node bears one leaf on alternate sides of the stem (see Fig. 2).

Annual A plant completing its life cycle within a single year, germinating from seed, flowering and setting seed itself, then dying.

Anther The portion of a stamen in which the pollen is formed (see Fig. 5).

Axil The place between a lateral branch of a stem, twig or leaf and the main stem.

Bearded With bristly hairs.

Berry A fleshy fruit, usually containing several seeds. Often used as a more general term for any fleshy fruit.

Biennial A plant which completes its life cycle in two years, developing a root and leaves in its first year, overwintering by means of food stored in the root, then flowering and setting seed in the second year, and dying.

Blade The expanded, flat portion of a leaf, in contrast to the stalk.

Bract A specialized leaf with a flower growing in its axil. Bracts may closely resemble leaves, or may differ in size, colour or texture, cf Spathe (see Fig. 1).

Bud An undeveloped flower or shoot protected by sepals (flower bud) or bud scales (shoot).

Bulb An extremely shortened underground stem with many swollen, fleshy leaves or leaf bases in which food is stored. Bulbs may or may not be enclosed in a protective tunic. They are common overwintering and food-storage organs in some monocotyledonous plants.

Bulbil A small bulb produced by some plants in the axils of leaves or in the inflorescence.

Calyx The sepals of a flower form the calyx. They are usually green and leaf-like, and enclose and protect the flower in bud. They may be joined or free, coloured or absent. In many families the calyx persists to enclose the fruit. In a calyx where the sepals are joined, the basal tubular portion is the calyx-tube, and the upper free parts are the calyx-lobes (see Fig. 5).

Capsule A dry fruit formed of several cells, which splits open to release the seeds.

Carpel One of the segments or cells which make up the ovary.

Claw The narrow basal section

Fig. 1 Parts of a Plant

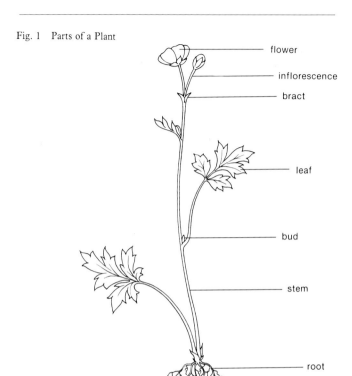

- flower
- inflorescence
- bract
- leaf
- bud
- stem
- root

of some petals and sepals.

Compound inflorescence A branched inflorescence composed of several racemes or cymes.

Compound leaf One which is composed of several leaflets (see Fig. 3).

Corm A short, erect, underground stem, swollen with food, often acting as an overwintering organ. It is often protected by a scaly tunic. The following year's corm develops on top of the spent one of the previous year.

Corolla The petals of a flower form the corolla. They are often coloured and conspicuous, and may bear nectaries, all features designed to attract insects. In some plants they are small, insignificant or absent (see Fig. 5).

Corona An additional structure between the petals and the stamens, such as the trumpet in daffodils.

Creeping With stems growing along the ground, rooting at the nodes.

Cyme A flat-topped or conical inflorescence in which the

Fig. 2   Leaf Arrangements

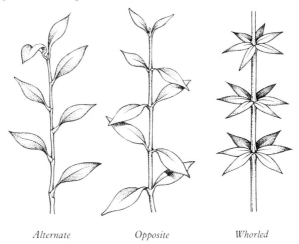

Alternate　　　　*Opposite*　　　　*Whorled*

branches develop equally from the centre, the central flower opening first in each branch. Each flower is the terminal one when it is formed (see Fig. 4).

Dehiscent Splitting open to release the seeds.

Disk The central portion of the flower head in a member of the Daisy family. It contains only tubular florets.

Dissected Of a leaf, one cut deeply into segments, and where the segments are themselves deeply cut (see Fig. 3).

Divided Of a leaf, cut into segments, the divisions extending as far as the midrib or the base, cf Lobed.

Drupe A fleshy fruit, usually with a single seed surrounded by a hard or stony layer.

Elliptical Of a leaf (see Fig. 3).

Entire Of a leaf, with an unbroken margin, not toothed (see Fig. 3).

Evergreen A plant that does not lose its leaves in winter.

Family A unit of biological classification consisting of a collection of genera sharing particular features, cf Genus.

Fertile Capable of reproduction; of a stamen, one produces pollen; of a flower, one producing viable seed.

Filament The stalk of a stamen (see Fig. 5).

Floret A single flower in the flower head of a member of the Daisy family. Disk florets are tubular, ray florets are strap-shaped. Flower heads may be composed wholly of disk florets or of ray florets, or may have disk florets in the centre and ray florets around the margin.

Follicle A dry, dehiscent fruit, opening along one side.

Free Not joined to other organs.

Fruit A ripened ovary which contains matured seeds, ready for dispersal.

Fused At least partially joined together, united.

Genus (plural Genera) A unit of biological classification consisting of a group of species considered to be related through common descent, and indicated by sharing the same first name, cf Species.

Gland An area on a plant which secretes a liquid, usually an oil or resin. When a plant has many glands, it is described as glandular; when the glands are situated on hairs, it is described as glandular-hairy.

Hair A small, usually slender outgrowth from a plant.

Head A dense flower cluster consisting of many stalkless flowers (see Fig. 5).

Herb A non-woody annual, biennial or perennial plant. If perennial, then dying back at the end of the season.

Herbaceous Having the texture of a herb; dying back to the ground each year.

Hermaphrodite Containing both male and female organs (stamens and carpels).

Hybrid A plant originating as a result of the cross between two species.

Indehiscent Of a fruit, not opening at maturity to release the seed(s).

Inferior Of an ovary, located beneath the other flower parts (see Fig. 5).

Inflorescence The flower cluster of a plant, including the branches, bracts and flowers (see Fig. 4).

Inserted The point of attachment, e.g. of stamens to the corolla.

Introduced Not native; having been brought to the country by man within historic times.

Involucre A set of bracts forming a structure like a calyx beneath an inflorescence. Often used specifically for the structure beneath the condensed head-like inflorescence of the members of the Daisy family.

Irregular Bilaterally symmetrical.

Lance-shaped Of a leaf (see Fig. 3).

Latex Milky juice or sap.

Legume A dry, dehiscent fruit characteristic of the Pea family. It opens along both sides to release the seeds.

Linear Of a leaf (see Fig. 3).

Lobed Of leaves, divided but with the divisions cutting less than halfway to the midrib. The leaves are therefore not divided into leaflets (see Fig. 3).

Membranous Flexible and thin, but usually not green.

Midrib The central vein of a leaf.

Mycorrhiza An association between the roots of certain plants and soil fungi. Orchids cannot survive without their mycorrhizal partners.

Fig. 3 Leaf Types

Simple Leaves

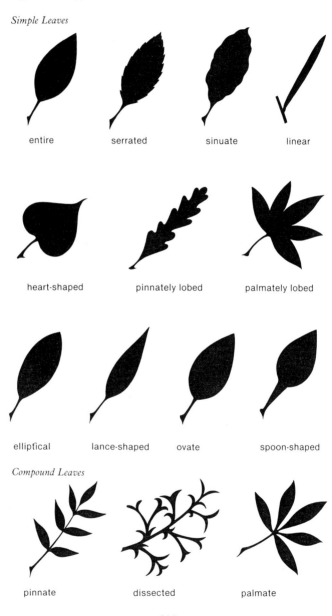

entire   serrated   sinuate   linear

heart-shaped   pinnately lobed   palmately lobed

elliptical   lance-shaped   ovate   spoon-shaped

Compound Leaves

pinnate   dissected   palmate

Native Endemic; not introduced by man.

Naturalized Well established and growing wild in an area, but coming from another region or part of the world.

Nectary A gland which secretes nectar, usually found on the receptacle or the petals of the corolla.

Node A point on a stem where leaves or roots, or both arise.

Nodule A small swelling.

Nutlet A small, dry, indehiscent fruit with a relatively thick wall and only one seed.

Opposite Two organs, such as leaves, growing opposite each other at a node (see Fig. 2).

Ovary The part of a flower which contains the ovules (see Fig. 5).

Ovate Of a leaf (see Fig. 3).

Ovule The structure which contains the egg. It develops into a seed after fertilization.

Palmate Of leaves, divided into three or more lobes or leaflets, all arising from the same point on the leaf stalk (see Fig. 3).

Pappus The crown of hairs, bristles or scales on the achene of a member of the Daisy family.

Parasite A plant which obtains its water and nutrients from another plant to which it becomes attached.

Perennial A plant which lives for several years, usually flowering each year, and (of herbaceous perennials) dying back at the end of the growing season.

Fig. 4   Inflorescence Types

Raceme

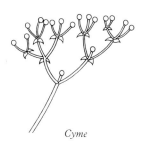

Cyme

Umbel

Head

Perianth The petals and sepals together.

Perianth segments The separate 'segments' which make up the perianth — they may be like petals or like sepals. This term is often used when all the parts of the perianth are similar and there is no clear division into sepals and petals.

Persistent Remaining attached to the fruit, especially of sepals or petals.

Petal One segment of the corolla. The petals are often brightly coloured and may have nectaries at the base (see Fig. 5).

Pinnate A compound leaf composed of more than three leaflets arranged in two rows on either side of the central axis or midrib (see Fig. 3).

Pod A dry, dehiscent fruit which opens along both sides. Usually used specifically to describe the fruits of the Pea family.

Pollen grains The structures which develop inside the anthers and which contain the male cells. They are carried to the stigma and there develop a pollen tube which grows down the style, carrying the male nucleus with it. When the pollen tube reaches the ovary, the male nucleus fuses with the ovule and the fertilized ovules develop into seeds.

Pollination The transfer of pollen from the anthers to the stigma, usually by wind or by insects.

Pome A fleshy fruit, the flesh derived from the receptacle and ovary wall, surrounding a tough inner layer, which in turn encloses the seeds, e.g. an apple.

Prickle A sharp outgrowth from a stem or leaf, but irregularly arranged, cf Spine.

Prostrate Lying flat on the ground.

Raceme An inflorescence with an elongated, unbranched central axis and flowers growing on stalks on each side. The lowermost flowers open first. In theory a raceme can go on elongating indefinitely as the youngest flowers are at the growing tip (see Fig. 4).

Receptacle The flat end of a flower stalk on which the various flower parts arise (see Fig. 5).

Regular Radially symmetrical.

Rhizome A perennial, underground stem growing horizontally. Rhizomes may act as an overwintering device, as a food storage organ, or as a method of spreading the plant.

Rosette A basal clump of leaves appearing to radiate outwards from a single spot.

Saprophyte A plant which lacks green colouring and which feeds on dead organic material, often with the help of mycorrhizal fungi.

Scale A thin, membranous bract or leaf.

Seed A ripened ovule.

Sepal One segment of the

Fig. 5   Parts of a Flower

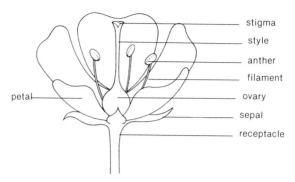

calyx. The sepals are usually green and leaf-like, and together they enclose and protect the flower bud (see Fig. 5).

Serrated Of a leaf, with a toothed margin where the teeth are pointed.

Siliqua A specialized capsule produced by members of the Mustard family; it has a central axis on which the seeds develop and two valves, one on each side of the axis. The valves open from the bottom upwards to release the seeds.

Simple leaf One with a single, undivided blade.

Sinuate Of a leaf, with a wavy margin (see Fig. 3).

Species A group of similar-looking individual plants which can interbreed and produce similar-looking offspring true to type.

Spike Strictly, a raceme in which the flowers lack stalks. In more general use, any spike-like inflorescence.

Spine A stiff, sharp-pointed projection from a plant, often a modified leaf or stipule, cf Prickle.

Spur A hollow, often slender projection from the base of a sepal or petal, usually containing nectar.

Stamen One of the male reproductive organs of a flower (see Fig. 5).

Sterile Incapable of producing viable pollen (of stamens) or seeds (of plants).

Stigma The receptive tip of the style on which pollen grains must land and adhere in order for pollination to occur (see Fig. 5).

Stipule An often leaf-like appendage found at the base of the leaf stalk where the stalk is attached to the stem. They often occur in pairs, one on each side of the stalk (see Fig. 1).

Style The stalk at the top of the ovary connecting it to the stigma where the pollen grains land (see Fig. 5).

Fig. 6　Flower Types

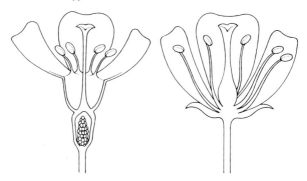

Flower with an inferior ovary　　*Flower with a superior ovary*

Superior Of an ovary, located above the other parts of a flower and free from them (see Fig. 5).

Tendril A climbing organ formed from part of a stem or leaf. In the Pea family, where tendrils are common, they are formed from the terminal leaflet of a compound leaf.

Ternate Of a leaf, divided into three equal leaflets; these in turn may also be divided.

Thallus The name given to the body of a plant when it is not clearly differentiated into stems and leaves, and often lacking roots.

Tuber A thickened portion of a root or rhizome acting as a food storage organ.

Tubercle A rounded swelling.

Tunic The dry, often brown and papery covering around a bulb or corm.

Turion A special winter bud produced by aquatic plants and by which they overwinter.

Umbel An umbrella-like inflorescence in which all the flower stalks arise from the same point on the stem (see Fig. 4).

Versatile A term used to describe an anther which is attached to the filament only at its middle, so that it is free to swing.

Weed A plant growing where it is not wanted.

Whorl A circle of three or more leaves or flowers growing from a node (see Fig. 2).

Xerophyte A plant adapted to life in a dry environment.

Index

(Figures in **bold** type indicate illustrations.)

Acknowledgements

The author and publisher would like to thank the libraries of the Natural History Museum, the Royal Horticultural Society, and the Linnean Society for their help.

RSNC

The Royal Society for Nature Conservation is pleased to endorse these excellent, fully illustrated pocket guide books which provide invaluable information on the wildlife of Britain and Northern Europe. Royalties from each book sold will go to help the RSNC's network of 48 Wildlife Trusts and over 50 Urban Wildlife Groups, all working to protect rare and endangered wildlife and threatened habitats. The RSNC and the Wildlife Trusts have a combined membership of 184,000 and look after over 1800 nature reserves. If you would like to find out more please contact the RSNC, The Green, Whitham Park, Lincoln, LN5 7NR. Telephone 0522 752326.